TENNIS LEGEND
Pancho Gonzalez

Doreen Gonzales

Published by Gregory Gonzales Publishing
Email: ggonzales28@cox.net

Printed in the United States of America

Illustration Credits: Courtesy of The International Tennis Hall of Fame &
Museum, Newport, R.I., pp. 6, 25, 39, 51, 63, 69, 79, 81, 85, 92, 93, 95, 98, 102, 105,
106, 109, 111, 117, 124; La Jolla Beach & Tennis Club pp. 42, 56, 64, 66, 67, 75;
Russell Corporation pp. 73, 115; Wally Parks NHRA Motorsports Museum p. 90

Special thanks to Joseph B. Stahl for his editorial suggestions and advice on
historical background.

Contents

To Donna,
my delightful sister.
Love,
Dorri

Richard "Pancho" Gonzalez receives a trophy from William "Slew" Hester at the Merion Cricket Club. He would receive many trophies during his long career.

The Best Player Ever

Richard Gonzalez stood ready—ready to fight for the most important thing in his life. It was September 5, 1949, and Gonzalez was at Forest Hills, New York, seconds away from starting the United States National Tennis Championships final.

Thirteen thousand spectators filled the stadium expecting to see one of the best tennis matches of the year. Gonzalez was not thinking about them though. His mind was focused on the man on the other side of the net—current Wimbledon champion and long-time rival, Ted Schroeder.

The match began. Both men fought fiercely for each point. The two seemed evenly matched as the lead kept changing hands. It took Schroeder one hour and thirteen minutes to beat Gonzalez in the first set, 18–16.

Between sets Schroeder put on spiked shoes for better traction on the grass court that had become slippery due to dampness. Gonzalez did not own spikes.[1] Schroeder quickly won the second set 6–2.

Then Gonzalez's friend Frank Shields pulled him aside. He told Gonzalez to move closer to the net when Schroeder was serving. Shields explained that he was playing too far back to make a forceful return. Gonzalez took the advice and promptly won the third and fourth sets.

Now the match score was tied at two sets apiece. The winner of the next set would win the U.S. National Championship. Gonzalez won the first game of it even though Schroeder was serving. This is called breaking serve. Breaking serve is so difficult it can destroy the server's self-confidence. Indeed, Schroeder weakened as Gonzalez continued attacking relentlessly. By the end of the ninth game, Gonzalez was leading 5–4.

Gonzalez opened the tenth game with a searing serve that flew past Schroeder untouched. This is known as an ace. The next several points seesawed back and forth. Then Gonzalez smashed a ball past Schroeder to go up by one point. If Gonzalez captured the next point, he would be the 1949 U.S. tennis champion.

Gonzalez served. Schroeder returned it. Gonzalez hit a shot deep into Schroeder's court. Schroeder responded by driving the ball down Gonzalez's sideline, and Gonzalez let it go. He believed the ball would fall out of bounds. Everyone looked to the linesman for the deciding call. When he signaled out-of-bounds, Richard Gonzalez became the 1949 tennis champion of the United States!

The crowd erupted in cheers. Gonzalez was jubilant! He ran to meet Schroeder and shake his hand. Cameras flashed as Gonzalez savored the moment.

This was Gonzalez's second U.S. championship title. But this one held a special meaning. Some people thought his first title win had been due to luck. Gonzalez knew better. He hoped this second national championship would prove to everyone that he was a true champion.

Gonzalez himself knew he belonged in championship tennis. He had an abundance of confidence that he backed up with hard work and superb talent. These traits would take Gonzalez to the top of the tennis world. Perseverance and determination would keep him there.

For ten years Gonzalez was the best tennis player in the world. This reign at the top lasted longer than that of any other player in history. Gonzalez won every professional tennis tour from 1954 to 1961 and a record eight U.S. Professional Championship titles. He was ranked among the World Top Ten players for more than twenty years. Even today, many people consider Richard Gonzalez the greatest tennis player who ever lived.

Gonzalez was different from other champions of his time. Many top players came from families that were financially comfortable. Most had received tennis lessons by at least as early as their teenage years. The lessons were usually taught in private clubs. And the clubs were all white.

Richard Gonzalez was none of these. He was a dark-skinned young man from a working class family. He was born in a small Los Angeles apartment to Mexican immigrants. Both his parents worked to support their family, and there was little money for extras like tennis lessons. Gonzalez had no lessons or coaches to help him along. He learned the sport mostly by watching others.

Even if Gonzalez's family had been rich, though, he probably would not have been allowed to join any private tennis clubs.[2] His skin was too dark. Discrimination against people of color was common when Gonzalez was growing up in the 1930s and 1940s. In his hometown of Los Angeles, Mexican-Americans were often the target of prejudice.

Gonzalez, however, rarely talked about prejudice. Instead, he channeled his energy and emotions into tennis. With talent and resolve, Gonzalez rose to become one of the first Latino superstar athletes in the world.

Gonzalez's father, Manuel Antonio Gonzales, was born in Mexico. Manuel's mother died when he was only eight years old. Soon after her death, Manuel and his father left Mexico. They walked 700 miles across the desert to an aunt's house in Globe, Arizona. One morning Manuel woke up and his father was gone. Manuel stayed with his aunt helping tend her farm. In the winter months he carried firewood for miles. He had a very hard childhood. He stayed with his aunt until he was in his teens. He then moved to Los Angeles, California.[3]

Manuel Gonzales was one of a half million Mexicans who immigrated into the U.S. from Mexico between 1900 and 1920. Most came to escape poverty or the revolutionary war that was then raging in their country. The majority of these immigrants settled in the Southwest and worked in factories and mines or on railroads, farms, and ranches.

Many of the immigrants could not read or write English, so U.S. officials wrote for them. This included spelling an immigrant's name. Officials frequently Americanized the Spanish spellings. This happened to Manuel Gonzales. In Mexico, his name was spelled with a "z" at the end—Gonzalez. In the U.S., though, the spelling became Gonzales.

Manuel Gonzales used the new spelling for the rest of his life. He passed it down to all of his children, including Richard. During the 1960s, though, Richard returned to the Spanish spelling of his last name.[4] This was an expression of pride in his heritage. As a result, Gonzalez's name is spelled differently in various books and articles, depending upon when they were written.

Richard Gonzalez's mother, Carmen, was also a Mexican immigrant. Her family had been wealthy and had owned a lot of land in

Manuel Gonzales walked 700 miles to Globe, Arizona, when he was a young boy.

Mexico. Carmen's family left the country when she was fourteen years old to escape the Mexican Revolution. They gave their land deeds to a lawyer-cousin for safekeeping and moved to Los Angeles. They planned to return when the war ended. While they were away, though, the trusted cousin betrayed them. He put their land in his own name and refused to give it back. With no property to go home to in Mexico, Carmen's family stayed in the U.S.[5]

Carmen met Manuel Gonzales when she was eighteen years old. She was a beautiful young woman with jet-black hair and dark brown eyes. She stood five-feet seven-inches tall. She and Manuel soon fell in love and were married. Their first child, Richard Alonzo, was born on May 9, 1928. In 1929, Carmen gave birth to twins,

**Carmen Gonzales's family in Mexico
was very wealthy.**

Manuel and Margaret. Ophelia (Terry), Bertha, Ralph, and Yolanda would follow.

The Gonzales family was not poor, but poverty was never far away. They lived in a succession of small houses in Central Los Angeles. Each one was on the outskirts of a poor neighborhood. As time passed, their home would become surrounded by poverty. Then Mr. and Mrs. Gonzales would move their family. They were determined to keep their children away from the crime that came with the poverty.

Carmen, Richard, Manuel, Terry, Bertha, and baby Ralph.

Unfortunately, they could never move far. They would settle into another modest house on the edge of another poor neighborhood. Again, the poverty would creep in around them, and again they would move. This pattern was repeated so many times in Richard's childhood that he later reported, "It was like a game of tag, and often we became tired of running."[6]

No matter where they lived, though, the Gonzales home was neat and well maintained. There was always food on the table. Often it was a simple meal of beans and tortillas. The children's clothes were simple too, and there were few luxuries in the Gonzales home.

Mr. Gonzales was a furniture finisher who also painted scenery for Hollywood movies. After laboring all day, he came home to garden or make repairs around the house. Richard later remembered his father's commitment to perfection, saying that Mr. Gonzales might tear something apart and put it back together fifteen times before he was satisfied that it was right.

Mrs. Gonzales worked as a seamstress. She often had cuts on her fingers from sewing machine needles. When she was not at work she cooked, cleaned, and cared for her children. Richard's overriding memory of his mother was of her dignity. She dressed with care and moved with a regal bearing. When she walked into a room she was treated with respect.

The Gonzales family spoke Spanish at home. When Richard entered kindergarten he began to learn English. English gradually replaced Spanish in the Gonzales household as the other children entered school. Mr. and Mrs. Gonzales encouraged this, knowing that English would help them succeed in the U.S. But they also felt it was important that their children speak proper Spanish. They wanted them to be proud of their Mexican heritage. So they continued to speak Spanish often.[7]

Richard and his younger brother Manuel.

Once, Mrs. Gonzales took Richard to a park to watch tennis. Tennis was a game she remembered seeing wealthy people play in Mexico. The outing reminded her of her own childhood when her family had been well off. These memories filled Mrs. Gonzales with joy. She was especially lighthearted and fun that day.

Six-year-old Richard noticed his mother's mood. He mistakenly believed it was due to her love of tennis. Hoping to make her happiness last forever, he told her, "Mama, someday I will be the best [tennis] player ever and you will be real happy."[8]

1 Hal Higdon, *Champions of the Tennis Court* (Englewood Cliffs, N.J.: Prentice-Hall, Inc., 1971), p.29.

2 Arthur R. Ashe, Jr., *A Hard Road To Glory: A History of the African-American Athlete* (New York: Amistad Press, Inc., 1993), p.146.

3 Rita Agassi Gonzalez, "The Power and the Fury," *World Tennis,* September 1987, p.26.

4 Interview with Richard Gonzalez's nephew, Gregory Gonzales, May 28, 2006.

5 R. Gonzalez, p.26.

6 Cy Rice, *Man With a Racket: The Autobiography of Pancho Gonzales* (New York: A. S. Barnes and Company, 1959), p.33.

7 R. Gonzalez, p.27.

8 Ibid., p.26.

He Could Overcome Anything

Young Richard was always very active. He went to the Los Angeles River often to skip rocks and catch frogs. He was handy, too. He liked to build toys and carve cars out of wood. He built stilts and pole vaults that he and his younger brothers and sisters played with. Whenever possible, Richard was outside.

Manuel Sr., Richard (right) and Manuel.

Prisoner was Richard's favorite game. It required speed, and speed was something the seven-year-old boy had in abundance. The object of Prisoner was to "capture" members of the opposing team. One day as the neighborhood kids played, Richard caught his brother Manuel. But Manuel broke loose and Richard threw a rock at him to stop him. The rock cut the back of Manuel's head, and Manuel ran home screaming as blood poured from the wound.

When Mr. Gonzales heard what Richard had done, he took his son to the garage and beat him with an electrical cord. Then he tied a string to each of Richard's thumbs and pulled his arms upward until they were straight over his head. He attached the strings to the ceiling of the garage and left Richard standing like that for three hours.[1]

This kind of punishment would be considered abusive by today's standards. Mr. Gonzales, however, did not feel he was being abusive. He felt he was being strict. He believed he needed to use these methods to discipline a rebellious son. Furthermore, Richard was the oldest child and Mr. Gonzales insisted he be an example to the younger children.[2] For this reason, Richard suffered through many harsh punishments in his childhood.

But Richard and his father had good times together, too. For instance, Mr. Gonzales taught his seven-year-old son how to shoot marbles. Marbles is played by flicking a large marble at several smaller ones that have been placed inside a circle. The object is to knock more small marbles outside the circle than one's opponent does.

Richard and Mr. Gonzales competed fiercely at marbles, both of them very serious about winning. Richard practiced constantly and before long he was beating his father. Mr. Gonzales then enlarged the playing circle to make it more difficult for his son to win. Undaunted, Richard practiced more.

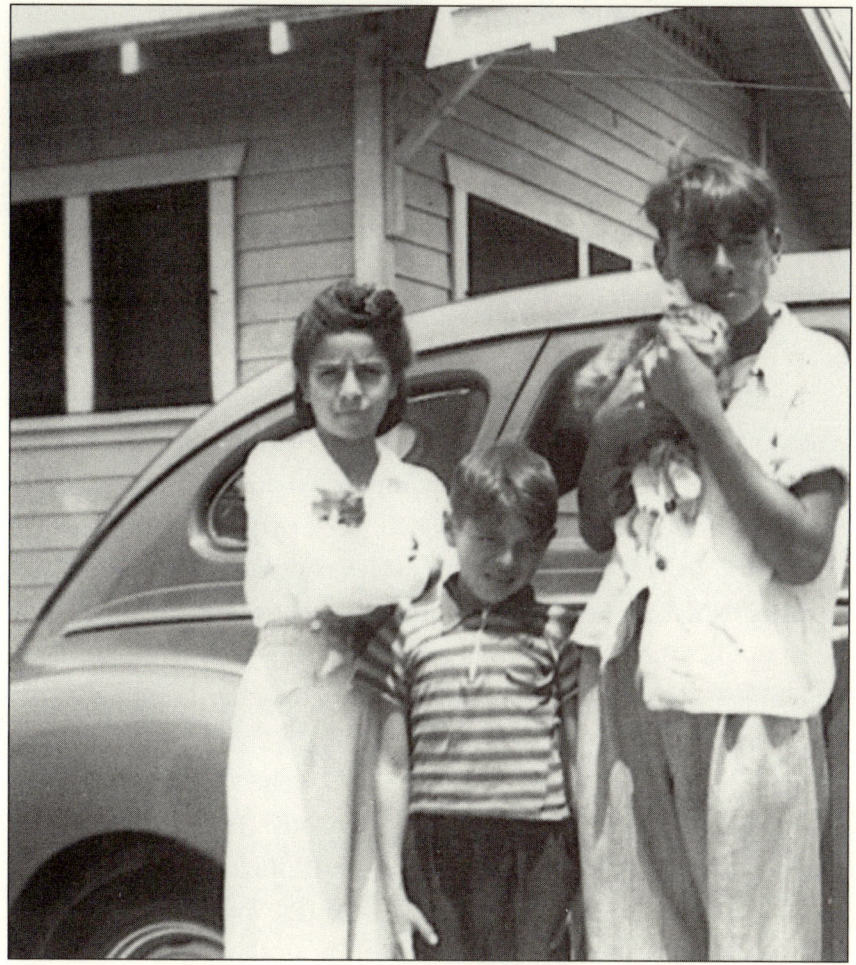

Richard (right) with siblings Terry and Ralph.

Richard played marbles at school, too. After a while there was no one left in his third grade class to conquer. So every recess Richard climbed over the fence that separated the younger pupils from the older ones. There he challenged the fourth, fifth, and sixth graders to marbles. He frequently won.

Seeking out more competition, Richard entered local marbles tournaments that were held at various Los Angeles parks. He and a friend often rode their homemade scooters to these contests. While on their way to one, Richard accidentally pushed his scooter in front of a moving car. The car's door handle smashed into his face and ripped his left cheek open. An ambulance rushed Richard to the hospital. Two weeks later he was back in the neighborhood playing—only now he had a large scar on his left cheek in the shape of an H.[3]

This accident did not prevent Richard from attending more marbles tournaments. He even won the Los Angeles city marbles championship once. Besides the thrill of competition, Richard went to these tournaments to watch a black man who gave exhibitions there.

This man was an excellent marbles shooter with a jovial personality. What made him extraordinary was the fact that he had no arms. He shot marbles by lying on his side and using his toes. Watching the man shoot marbles convinced Richard that he "could overcome anything."[4]

Young Richard was not only determined, he was bright. He was a quick learner and his grades were excellent. He liked school and never missed a day of elementary school. Richard even went to school when he was sick because he did not want to stay in bed. Due to his intelligence and excellent attendance, Richard was allowed to skip fourth grade. In 1937, he moved directly from third grade to fifth.

In junior high, Richard joined his school football and basketball teams. He did well on both. Mrs. Gonzales, however, worried that her active son would get hurt. When he asked for a bike for Christmas, she gave him something she thought would be safer. Mrs. Gonzales gave Richard a tennis racket she had purchased at a discount store for fifty-one cents. In addition to diverting her twelve-year-old son from rough activities, Mrs. Gonzales hoped the game would expose him to some of the finer things in life.

At the time, Los Angeles had one of the best private tennis facilities in the world, the Los Angeles Tennis Club. This club was a fancy place, complete with restaurant, bar, locker rooms, and professional players to give lessons.

Mr. and Mrs. Gonzales could not afford to give Richard lessons at the Los Angeles Tennis Club. And even if they could have, Richard would probably not have been admitted. His Mexican heritage most likely would have kept him out.[5]

Actually, Mr. and Mrs. Gonzales could not afford tennis lessons anywhere. This did not stop Richard from learning the sport. Every day he walked to a nearby park to watch people play tennis. By watching and listening to others Richard learned the rules and sometimes confusing scoring system.

A tennis match is really a series of several games. Both players begin at zero, a score that is called love. Each game consists of four points: 15, 30, 40, and the game-winning point. The same player serves an entire game, and when the score is announced, the server's score is always said first. When one player fails to hit a ball into the court on the other side of the net, the other earns a point. But each game must be won by at least two points. For example, if both players win three points, the score is tied at 40–all. This is also called deuce. To win this game, a player must get ahead by two points. The player who wins the first of the next two points is said to have "ad." This stands for advantage, for if he wins the next point, he wins the game. If he loses the next point, the score returns to deuce. This continues until someone wins the game.

When one game is finished, it is the other player's turn to serve. The player who wins six games first wins that set of games. But a set must also be won by two games. Therefore, a set score of 6–5 would

Richard's parents Manuel and Carmen.

make it necessary to play at least one more game. When both players are evenly skilled, a set sometimes continues for a long time with
the lead alternating after each game. Today, most tournaments have

tie-breaks when a set reaches 6–6. This brings a quick finish to this kind of a set.

Yet the end of a set is still not the end of a tennis contest. Tennis matches consist of a predetermined number of sets. Players most often compete for either the best of three sets or the best of five sets.

Richard learned the scoring system and the rules through observation. He was not the only one. Most other Mexican-Americans and African-Americans had to learn the rules on their own, too. This meant that only the most determined people of color would learn to play tennis. Richard clearly belonged in this category.

Not long after his mother gave him his first racket, Richard realized he had fallen in love with tennis. He was at the park whenever possible, and he was always looking for someone to challenge to a match. When no one was available, he played alone, practicing his serve.

Richard with his tennis racket.

Richard's tennis racket became his constant companion, and he took it everywhere he went—even to bed! Sometimes he prayed before going to sleep, asking God to help him become a great tennis player.

One day Richard began watching tennis practice at a nearby high school. He struck up a friendship there with a member of the school's team, Charles "Chuck" Pate. Pate called Richard "Pancho," a nickname that Richard did not mind coming from his friend.

Before long, Richard was helping Pate with his morning newspaper route. In exchange, Pate gave Richard tennis lessons. Pate taught Richard the proper way to hit forehand and backhand strokes. The forehand stroke is hit with the face of the hand swinging the racket into the ball. The back of the hand swings into the ball on the backhand stroke. Pate also showed Richard the correct way to serve.

Richard supplemented Pate's instructions by studying good players' methods and styles and imitating them. As he did, he began developing a style that would mark his tennis game for the rest of his life.

One of the first skills Richard mastered was a hard serve. This may have been because it was the part of the game that Richard could practice alone.

During a tennis match, a player has two chances to serve the ball over the net and into the correct area of an opponent's court, which is called the service box. A player's first missed serve is called a fault. The second one is called a double fault. A double fault gives the opponent a point. When a player serves the ball so hard that a player cannot even make contact with it, the server is said to have aced the opponent.

Richard's serves became the hardest around, and he often aced other players. Even when he did not ace them, he rarely faulted on the first serve. A double fault by Richard was practically nonexistent.

Through hard practice Richard developed a great serve.
Here he is shown playing Australia's Ken Rosewall
in the horseshoe Stadium at Forest Hills.

Furthermore, Richard was quick. He could move across a tennis court faster than other players. His large size gave him an added advantage in covering ground. Richard would eventually grow to six-foot three-inches tall. As a youth, he had a good start. With a longer stride and longer reach than many young people, Richard could return shots other players could not even reach.

It did not take Richard long to wear out the nylon strings in his first racket. Within a month of receiving the gift, he was repairing it with pliers, nails, and new string. His handiwork extended the life of his first racket, enabling him to enter the city's public tennis tournament. Soon Richard was carrying a first place ribbon home to his proud mother.

Richard's father was not as excited. Mr. Gonzales believed that tennis was a sport for the idle rich. As far as he was concerned, tennis had no place in Richard's life. It would not help him succeed or earn money.[6]

In one way, Mr. Gonzales was right. At the time, very few people earned a living by playing tennis. Those who did were the world's best players and most had wealthy sponsors.

Perhaps Richard's father was thinking of another obstacle—racism. Racism was something young Richard did not know much about. His life revolved around his home, neighborhood, and school. Since the people in these settings were mostly Mexican-American, Richard experienced no ethnic discrimination. In many ways, he grew up sheltered from racism.[7]

Although Richard had little experience with prejudice against Mexican-Americans, it did exist. For example, some Los Angeles swimming pools only admitted Mexican-Americans on certain days, and entire neighborhoods barred Mexican-Americans from moving into them.[8]

Yet Mr. and Mrs. Gonzales rarely spoke about racism with their children. Instead, they taught them to be proud of their heritage. One of Richard's brothers later remembered how his parents often told their children, "You're Mexican. You want to walk with your head high."[9]

In fact, when Richard first became aware of discrimination, it puzzled him. He could not understand why someone would judge him because of his heritage. He asked his grandmother about the strange concept. She told Richard that he had been lucky to escape discrimination in his life. But, she went on, someday it would appear. "Perhaps when you ask for a job," she said, "or the look in a policeman's eyes... the glances in the stores. It is worse in the heat of anger, when someone denounces you—calls you a Mexican and makes it sound ugly."[10]

Richard's grandmother offered him some advice. She told him to remain calm whenever anyone insulted him. Then, she said, he should imagine that person in his or her underwear. This mental image would make Richard laugh and the hateful words would sting less. It would be years before Richard used her advice.

In the meantime, he continued playing tennis. One of his favorite places to play was Exposition Park. This public park had eight hard-surface tennis courts where many talented players, including Mexican-Americans and African-Americans, gathered.

Next to the courts was a small tennis store called the Exposition Park Tennis Shop. It was run by Frank Poulain. Poulain soon noticed that Richard had a natural talent for the game. He was convinced that Richard had the makings of a champion. So Poulain helped him get equipment and encouraged him to practice and develop his skills.

Poulain was not the only one who saw talent in Richard. A sales representative from an athletic supply company saw him play and

Frank Poulain at Exposition Park courts. Richard is in the background.

gave him two new rackets as free samples. Richard was thrilled with the gift and immediately tried out the rackets. In his excitement, he stayed out an hour past his curfew. When he arrived home that night Mr. Gonzales was furious. He beat Richard with a belt. Throughout the beating, Richard hugged his new rackets close to his chest to protect them.

"When I tell you to be home at a certain time you will be home!", his father raged. "If you think you are going to do what you please, you will be taught a lesson! You live in my house and you will do what I say! Tennis is for bums! You will not be a bum! Give me those!"[11]

Before Richard could stop him, Mr. Gonzales had pried a racket loose and broke it over his knee. "Go ahead!" Richard screamed in defiance. "Break the other! I'll be back with two more!"[12] The boy was true to his word. When the salesman heard what had happened, he gave Richard another racket to replace the broken one.

Early in high school Richard gave up all other sports to concentrate on tennis. This did not surprise the people who knew Richard. As one of his sisters would later remember, Richard always wanted to be the best at whatever he did.

Tennis and Richard were a good match. There was no standing around between plays like in football; no one to throw the ball to as in basketball. Tennis was nothing but pure action. It had to be won by one strong, quick and smart player all by himself. The sport seemed tailor-made for Richard.

During his school lunch break, Richard often went out to practice tennis. One day he stayed outside the whole afternoon working on his various shots. That day's hooky playing was the beginning of a pattern.

Richard would ride all over the city on his bicycle.

Soon Richard was spending more time on the tennis court than in the classroom. Then he was dodging truant officers that the school sent out to find him. As an adult, he once said that he covered more ground running from school officials than he did playing in a tennis tournament.

Not surprisingly, Richard's attendance habits did not sit well with his father. School, not tennis, Mr. Gonzales insisted, was the road to success. So Richard pursued his passion without his father's support. This included finding his own way to tournaments. Usually he rode his bicycle. As an adult Richard Gonzalez recalled that this had been a terrific way to train. "[I] didn't have to worry about my legs being in shape," he said. "I'd ride all over the city. I'd go 15 to 20 miles a day and not give it a thought."[13]

While Richard bicycled from one public court to another, a talented youngster named Herb Flam was fine-tuning his own tennis game at the Los Angeles Tennis Club. Flam was from Beverly Hills, a wealthy area of Los Angeles, and had been taking lessons for years.

Throughout 1942, Flam was considered the best young player in Southern California. In fact many people thought Flam just might be the top player in his age group in the country.

Flam and Richard met on the court for the first time in 1943. While many people knew Flam, few had heard of Richard Gonzalez. Even fewer expected the Mexican-American youth to win. But he did!

Richard continued winning local tournaments and beating Flam. By the end of 1943, the self-taught Mexican-American teenager from a working-class home was ranked the number one boy under fifteen years of age in Southern California. Just as important as being ranked number one, though, was being noticed by Perry T. Jones.

Jones's official job title was secretary and tournament manager of the Southern California Tennis Association (SCTA). But Jones was better known for finding and developing young tennis players in Southern California. He was so good at nurturing future champions that some people referred to the Association as the "Perry Jones tennis factory."

Jones had the power to make or break a young tennis player. He decided whether or not a certain youngster had enough talent to receive instruction and financial help from the Association. Jones made sure that promising youth received the finest coaching available at the tennis club, often learning from practice with world champions. The best young players were invited to important California tournaments. The very best were sent to tournaments all around the country at the Association's expense.

Until Richard's 1943 victories over Flam, Flam had been Jones's most promising future star. Now there was a new star rising. This star, however, would receive no help from the SCTA. Perry Jones told Richard that in order to play in SCTA tournaments, a boy had to go to school.

Richard was stubborn. He refused to attend school, so he was barred from Association tournaments. Without tennis tournaments to keep him challenged, he looked for other kinds of excitement. Unfortunately, one was illegal. In 1943, Richard was convicted of burglary. As a result, Richard was sentenced to spend several months at a juvenile correctional facility.[14] Now Richard's days were filled with classes and work. There were no tennis courts at the facility and no time to play anyway.

Upon his release in 1944, Richard remained banned from Association tournaments. Some people felt that Jones was enforcing his "no school, no competition" rule simply because Richard was Mexican-American. Jones denied this charge. He said that if Richard returned to school as a serious student, he would be welcomed back into tournaments. He added, "It isn't fair for [Richard] to practice tennis all day while the other youngsters are in school."[15]

Yet some young players did have shortened school schedules arranged for them by Mr. Jones and the SCTA. For example, one star, Jack Kramer, went to classes in the morning and spent each afternoon at the Los Angeles Tennis Club taking lessons and practicing with world champions. But no one had ever offered Richard this kind of an arrangement. Instead, he was left with a flat ultimatum— no school, no tennis.

Richard quit school anyway. He was only sixteen years old and had only completed tenth grade. His friends told him this was a bad idea. His mother pleaded with him to finish high school. Mr. Gonzales forbad him to drop out. Richard quit anyway.

He would regret this decision for the rest of his life. Even when tennis brought him wealth and fame, he still wished he had completed high school and college.

Mrs. Gonzales also regretted her son's decision. After Richard won his first national championship, one reporter asked her what she thought of her son's achievement. She answered that she would rather have seen him graduate from high school and college.

At age sixteen, though, playing tennis was the only thing Richard was interested in doing. Unfortunately, he was banned from the most important tournaments in the area. Such banishment would have brought an end to most teenagers' dreams of glory. Richard, however, was not like most young people.

---

1 Rita Agassi Gonzalez, "The Power and the Fury," *World Tennis*, September 1987, p.26.
2 Ibid., p.27.
3 *Current Biography Yearbook*, 1949 (New York: H. W. Wilson, 1949), p.230.
4 R. Gonzalez, p.26.
5 Himilce Novas, *The Hispanic 100: A Ranking of the Latino Men and Women Who Have Most Influenced American Thought and Culture* (New York: A Citadel Press Book, 1995), p.231.
6 Elizabeth Bennett, "Pancho Gonzales," *Houston Post*, July 28, 1987.
7 Cy Rice, *Man With a Racket: The Autobiography of Pancho Gonzales* (New York: A. S. Barnes and Company, 1959), p.134.
8 Peter Skerry, *Mexican Americans: The Ambivalent Minority* (New York: MacMillan, 1993), p.23.

9 Paul Bauman, "Gonzalez's Talent Matched By Tenacity," *Las Vegas Review-Journal,* July 5, 1995, p.3E.

10 Rice, p.134.

11 R. Gonzalez, p.77.

12 Ibid.

13 Andrea Leand, "The Lone Wolf," *Tennis Week,* July 20, 1995, p.12.

14 RaymondLee, "TheNatural," *TennisWeek,* (March15,2006) *http://www.sportsmediainc. net/tennisweek/index.cfm?func=showarticle&newsid=1062414.*

15 Gene Farmer, "Pancho Gonzales," *Life,* June 6, 1949, p.71.

Richard's parents at church.

Climbing

Richard was happy. Now he could spend all his time playing tennis. When he was not on the court, he was in Frank Poulain's Tennis Shop talking about the sport.

Soon, though, Richard began to understand that he had eliminated himself from meaningful competition. Yet he still refused to go to school. With few choices, Richard enlisted in the United States Navy in the fall of 1945.[1]

He spent most of the next year and a half on a transport ship in the Pacific Ocean. He performed maintenance tasks such as scrubbing the ship's deck. Gonzalez did not like the Navy. It had too many rules and regulations. Worse still, he could not play tennis. So as soon as he was discharged in January 1947, Gonzalez returned to his home in Los Angeles and his second home at Exposition Park.

Mr. Gonzales told his eighteen-year-old son that he had three choices. He could go to school, get a job, or leave home. Gonzalez packed his clothes and tennis rackets and headed for Poulain's shop. For the next couple of weeks he stayed there, sleeping on a sofa in

Manuel Sr., Margaret, Richard in uniform, and Carmen.

the back of the store. Finally, Mr. Gonzales resigned himself to his son's determination to play tennis and let him move back home.

While Gonzalez had been floating around the Pacific, his old rival Herb Flam had been winning tennis tournaments all around the country, capturing the National Junior Championship twice.

Area experts believed he would place well in an upcoming men's tournament, the Southern California Championships. Jack Kramer was expected to win the tournament. Kramer, in fact, was the current U.S. champion.

As for Gonzalez, he had not even received an invitation to the California tournament. This was not surprising. Gonzalez had only been on the tennis scene for a short while before being suspended because of his poor school attendance. He had then served time in juvenile detention and then joined the Navy. So it had been three years since he had been active in Southern California tennis.

But now Gonzalez was back, and he was about to let the tennis world know it. He promptly sent in an entry form to the tournament, hoping to be accepted.

When Perry Jones received Gonzalez's application, he did not want to let him enter. However, Gonzalez's supporters argued that since he was an adult, Jones could not keep him out. So Gonzalez entered the tournament.

Tennis tournaments proceed through several rounds of play. They are usually single elimination affairs, meaning that as soon as a player loses a match, he is out of the tournament. The winning player advances to the tournament's next round. Once more the losers are eliminated and the winners move on. When only two players are left, a final match decides the tournament winner.

Before a tournament begins, the best players are seeded (ranked according to their ability). For example, the person the organizers think will win the tournament is seeded number one. The player who is expected to come in second is seeded number two, and so on. Seeded players are not scheduled to compete against each other until the tournament's later rounds. This system keeps good players from eliminating each other in the early rounds of the tournament.

As one of the best players in California, Flam was seeded in this Southern California Championship, but Gonzalez was not. However, in each of his matches Gonzalez worked his way a little closer to the final round. Gonzalez advanced until his name was placed opposite Flam's.

On the morning of this important match, Gonzalez filled his athletic bag with his freshly ironed T-shirt and a pair of tennis shorts. His mother wished him luck, and he walked out of the house feeling confident. It took Gonzalez three streetcars to get to the Los Angeles Tennis Club, but he arrived there in plenty of time.

Gonzalez looked over the spectators while he waited for his match to begin. He recognized a few movie stars. More important to Gonzalez, though, were the friends from Exposition Park who had come to cheer him on.[2] Frank Poulain and Chuck Pate were among them.

The stands were filled for Gonzalez's contest with Flam. Some people had been watching Gonzalez in the early rounds and had come back to watch him play Flam. Many anticipated an exciting contest between these two who were the best young players on the West Coast. And they were not disappointed.

When the first set ended, Flam had beaten Gonzalez 10–8. But as the match wore on, Flam could not handle Gonzalez's lightning serve. Gonzalez took the second set 8–6. With the score tied one set-all, the winner of the third set would win the match. When Gonzalez beat Flam 6–4, he knocked the brightest West Coast hopeful out of the tournament.

Now Gonzalez advanced to play Jack Kramer. No one expected Gonzalez to win, and he did not. Kramer beat him, 6–2, 6–4, 3–6, 6–3. In one sense, though, Gonzalez was victorious. During the contest, he aced Kramer six times. He even won a set from Kramer, something that only a few players had done all that year. Gonzalez was happy

**Gonzalez's determination and skill earn him a place on the
1947 Eastern grass-court circuit.**

with his performance. Although Kramer won the tournament, he felt
he had proven himself to be a top contender in amateur tennis.[3]

Even Perry Jones agreed. He immediately offered Gonzalez a
chance to go play tournaments on the Eastern grass-court circuit. He
invited Gonzalez on an expense-paid trip sponsored by the SCTA to

compete against the country's best players. If Gonzalez did well, he would earn national attention. Excited and hopeful, Gonzalez packed his bags. He did not intend to waste this golden opportunity.

**Gonzalez (first step) on his way to compete
on the Eastern grass-court circuit.**

The tour did give Gonzalez good exposure and experience. Yet in one way it was disappointing. Gonzalez often felt like an outsider among his teammates from the Los Angeles Tennis Club. He later remembered that while the more experienced players ignored him, they seemed generous with their advice to other rookies. "I felt that I should have had more support from those guys," he once said.[4] After all, Gonzalez reasoned, they were all representing Southern California.

But Gonzalez had not wasted his time in the East. He had watched and listened carefully, learning what he could through observation and experience. For example, most of the tournaments in the East at that time were played on grass courts. Gonzalez had never played on grass before. He quickly learned that a ball skids low across sod instead of bouncing up sharply like it does on concrete.

So although the snubbing left Gonzalez feeling excluded, he played well. He also became more widely known on the national tennis scene.

Furthermore, Gonzalez made some important new friends. For instance, in New York he met Frank Shields, an American tennis champion from the 1930s. Shields would give Gonzalez crucial support in the months ahead.

In addition, Gonzalez turned Perry Jones into an admirer. Jones was impressed by Gonzalez's aggressive style on the court. He was also impressed by his integrity. Once Jones accidentally sent Gonzalez an expense check for ninety-eight dollars too much. Although no one would have known if Gonzalez had kept it, he promptly returned the overpayment. This simple act of honesty endeared Gonzalez to Jones for years to come.[5]

In September 1947, Gonzalez made his first appearance at the United States National Championships. This tournament was played at the West Side Tennis Club in Forest Hills, New York. The

**Perry T. Jones awards Gonzalez a trophy. Jones would
eventually become an admirer and advocate of Gonzalez.**

top-seeded player there that year was Jack Kramer. Frankie Parker
was seeded number two and Gardnar Mulloy number three. In his
premier outing at the U.S.'s most prestigious amateur tournament,
Gonzalez played so well that he almost beat Mulloy.

When Gonzalez returned to Los Angeles, he played in the
Pacific Southwest Tournament. There he defeated Czechoslovakian
Jaroslav Drobny, the number-five-ranked player in the world, and
Parker, the number three-ranked. But in the next round, Gonzalez
lost to Schroeder.

Gonzalez's successes brought him new attention. With this
attention came closer scrutiny, and tennis fans soon saw that he was

different from other players. First of all, he was Mexican-American. Second, he was not the socially sophisticated young man that many people assumed tennis players to be. Gonzalez smoked cigarettes and played poker. He often stayed out until the early hours of the morning. He enjoyed an occasional beer. At times, he seemed a little too relaxed as he sat courtside waiting to play.

Sports reporters noticed Gonzalez too. They wrote about his cannonball serve, his dynamic style at the net, and his attacking style in conquering an opponent. They also reported that Gonzalez had an easygoing, relaxed outlook on training. Some people saw these comments as thinly disguised references to the "lazy Mexican" stereotype. Whether these were racist comments or not, Gonzalez found himself in a world where his ethnic and working-class background stood out.

Gonzalez later recalled that it was at this point that he began seeing the subtle but definite edges of racism. For example, he often heard spectators commenting about the deep scar on his cheek. Many people assumed it had been caused in a knife fight. According to Gonzalez, some people believed that "a knife scar and a Mexican-American youth go hand in hand."[6] In fact, one radio program even broadcast an entirely made-up skit in which Gonzalez was in a fight and received this scar from a knife wound.

At the time, African-Americans often encountered more direct forms of racism in tennis. Many were openly barred from tournaments, no matter how talented they were. For example, although Oscar Johnson had won the Pacific Coast junior title every year from 1946–1948, he was told he could not play in a St. Louis tournament because he was an African-American. When Johnson and his lawyer challenged the decision, he was admitted. Even so, excluding African-Americans from tennis tournaments remained a common practice across the U.S.[7]

By the end of 1947, Gonzalez was ranked the seventeenth best player in the U.S. He had earned this ranking by playing well in ten different tournaments around the country. Unfortunately, Gonzalez had unknowingly broken a United States Lawn Tennis Association (USLTA) rule.

The USLTA was the organization that regulated amateur tennis in the U.S. It allowed American amateurs to accept expense money for only eight tournaments a year. Any more than that would make a player a professional. The distinction between amateurs and professionals was an important one.

Amateurs were not allowed to make money from tennis. They could not win prizes, endorse products, or give lessons. The only money amateurs could receive for tennis was the money it cost them to attend tournaments. Professionals, on the other hand, could make money from the sport. They could earn championship purses, be paid to advertise products, or coach.

At that time being a professional had drawbacks. Professionals were not allowed to enter the most prestigious tennis tournaments in the world. For example, the four most important national championships—those of the United States, France, Australia, and Great Britain (Wimbledon), were closed to professionals. These "Big Four" events are known as the "Grand Slam" tournaments. Someone who wins all four in one year is said to have won a Grand Slam. This is an extraordinary feat, performed by only a handful of people in tennis history.

Furthermore, professionals could not compete in international team contests. The most esteemed of these was, and still is, the Davis Cup competition. In this competition, players compete on national teams, and it is considered an honor to play for one's country.

In 1947, the USLTA board met to decide on Gonzalez's amateur status. Perry Jones went to the meeting to defend Gonzalez. He described him as a wonderful and dignified young man.[8] Jones convinced the board that an appropriate penalty for Gonzalez would be suspension from tournament play from February to June of 1948.

Gonzalez's penalty would keep him out of tennis for several months. However, the most important U.S. tournaments were held after June, and Gonzalez would be allowed to participate in these. Of course, Gonzalez did not sit around waiting for his suspension to end. He practiced daily. He also developed a new interest. Her name was Henrietta Pedrin.

Gonzalez met the seventeen-year-old at one of his sister's parties. The five-foot one-inch, ninety-eight pound beauty made his heart pound. Gonzalez took Henrietta on a date the very next evening, and from then on they were constant companions. Each afternoon Henrietta watched Gonzalez practice tennis. At night they went dancing.

Two months later, Gonzalez asked Henrietta to marry him. She said yes. But both knew their parents would be against the marriage. Henrietta was very young, and Gonzalez was supposed to be giving tennis his full attention. So one day in March, the two drove to Arizona where they were married quickly and quietly. They kept their wedding a secret and returned to their parents' homes as if nothing had changed.

Then one day Henrietta's mother decided that her daughter was spending too much time with Gonzalez. When Gonzalez came to pick her up, Mrs. Pedrin informed him that her daughter was staying home. Gonzalez was so upset he let the secret out. He told Mrs. Pedrin that he had a right to see his own wife.[9]

The newlyweds then moved into a small apartment and lived on expense money Gonzalez had saved from his tennis travels. The money did not go far. So when the Mexican government approached him with a unique offer, Gonzalez was interested.

Mexican officials wanted Gonzalez to play tennis for Mexico. If he would become a Mexican citizen, the officials told him, the government would pay for a college education and give Gonzalez money to travel around the world to play tennis. Furthermore, the government would guarantee Gonzalez a lifelong job at the Mexican consulate in Los Angeles.

This was an attractive offer to a young man who knew he wanted to spend his life playing tennis but had no way to finance this dream. Gonzalez thought about the offer for several weeks. Then a friend inadvertently helped him make up his mind. The friend asked Gonzalez if he would rather be on a Mexican or United States Davis Cup team. Suddenly, Gonzalez's answer was crystal clear. There was only one nation he wanted to represent in international play—the United States.[10] That settled the matter.

As soon as his suspension was lifted, Gonzalez was back on the courts in tournament action. In Chicago, he walked away with the first place trophy in the National Clay Court Championships. Next he won the state championships of both California and New Jersey.

At the end of 1947, Jack Kramer had made a monumental announcement—he was turning professional. This news sent the amateur world scrambling. With Kramer out of the picture, there were several players capable of winning the 1948 U.S. Championship, and Richard Gonzalez believed he was one of them.[11]

Throughout the summer, Gonzalez had been watching the other top players closely. He had made mental notes of their weaknesses and mentally filed the information away. He hoped he would get a chance to use it at the U.S. National Championships in September.

But most people were betting on Ted Schroeder to win the title. Schroeder had won the U.S. Championship in 1942, and many felt he was reaching his peak.

Gonzalez had already lost to Schroeder several times in various tournaments. According to Gonzalez, Schroeder had some kind of a psychological hold over him. Whenever the two met in a locker room before a match, Schroeder's boastful remarks to Gonzalez deflated his morale. Gonzalez claimed this made him play poorly. He knew that Schroeder would be an obstacle to his dreams of glory at Forest Hills.

Then Schroeder decided not to enter the 1948 national tournament. Now Gonzalez was positive he could take the title.

Not many people agreed. Most tennis experts were accustomed to watching their stars grow from childhood. This was only the second season Gonzalez had played in major competition, so to them he was a novice. Talented or not, many believed that it took years for championship players to develop. Few believed that Gonzalez would even make it to the final match.

Tournament officials seemed to feel the same. They seeded Gonzalez at only number eight. But all the experts in the world could not stifle Gonzalez's burning ambition. He left for Forest Hills in September, confident that he would return to Los Angeles as the U.S. amateur tennis champion.

---

1 Andrea Leand, "The Lone Wolf," *Tennis Week*, July 20, 1995, p.12.
2 Cy Rice, *Man With a Racket: The Autobiography of Pancho Gonzales* (New York: A. S. Barnes and Company, 1959), p.25–26.
3 "Mañana Comes," *Time*, May 19, 1947, p.50.
4 Leand, p.13.
5 *Current Biography Yearbook*, 1949 (New York: H. W. Wilson, 1949), p.231.
6 Rice, p.61.
7 Arthur R. Ashe, Jr., *A Hard Road To Glory: A History of the African-American Athlete* (New York: Amistad Press, Inc., 1993), p.146.
8 Gene Farmer, "Pancho Gonzales," *Life*, June 6, 1949, p.72.
9 Rice, p.72.
10 "Lazy, But Wonderful," *Newsweek*, August 2, 1948, p.70.
11 Ibid.

The Gonzalez backhand.

United States Champion

Gonzalez was on his own at the national tournament. He had no coach telling him what to do and no trainer overseeing his conditioning. He could practice or not, develop a strategy or not—the choice was his. The only advice he received came from his new friend, Frank Shields. Shields told Gonzalez to play hard for every point. He did.

In the quarterfinal round Gonzalez beat the number-one seed, Parker, a former U.S. and French champion. He then advanced to the semifinals where he would meet Jaroslav Drobny. The other semifinal match was between South Africa's Eric Sturgess and Herbie Flam. Gonzalez believed that he could beat Flam if the two met in the final.[1] First, though, Gonzalez had to beat Drobny, a great champion who eventually won the French and Wimbledon championships.

Drobny played well and won the first set, 10–8. But then, in what one writer called a dazzling exhibition of speed and power, Gonzalez won the next three sets to win the match. In the meantime, Sturgess beat Flam setting up a final round match between Richard Gonzalez and Eric Sturgess.

Spectators packed the stadium at Forest Hills on September 19, 1948, eager to witness the Gonzalez-Sturgess match. Gonzalez stepped onto the court hungry for victory. He took the first set, 6–2. Then he won the second set, 6–3. Gonzalez and Sturgess exchanged leads several times in the third set until the score was 13–12, Gonzalez.

As evening descended on the court, officials decided it was getting too dark to play. They told Gonzalez and Sturgess that they could play one more game. If this did not decide the contest, the match would be finished the next day. A proverb flashed through Gonzalez's mind—never put off until tomorrow what you can do today. Gonzalez won the next game to claim the third set and the United States National Championship!

Suddenly, Richard Gonzalez was the most popular tennis player in the nation. Articles about him appeared in *The New York Times* newspaper and in *Time* and *Life* magazines. Each one emphasized that no one had ever risen to the top so quickly. As the *Times*'s tennis writer Allison Danzig put it, "The rankest outsider of modern times sits on the tennis throne today."[2]

Gonzalez was unique in other ways, too. He had a distinctive playing style that many writers compared to the movements of a jungle cat. He crouched low in preparation for his opponent's shots. When one came, he pounced on the ball with great fury. But it was Gonzalez's serve that received the most attention. Enthusiasts described it as a rocket.

Gonzalez's style created excitement among spectators. No one could tell what would happen in a Gonzalez match. Wondering if he would make an inexplicable error or hit a brilliant shot, people leaned forward in their seats to watch him play. Gonzalez him-

After he won the National Championship in 1948, Gonzalez rose to fame. Many tennis fans were charmed by his intensity on the court and by his good looks.

self called his game unpredictable. "Sometimes my forehand is my weakness," he explained, and, "sometimes my backhand. It all depends on how I'm feeling that day."[3]

Fans also found the new champion's background intriguing. Some writers characterized him as rebellious and emphasized his truancy during high school. This soon earned him the title of the bad boy of tennis. In a world that presented its champions as well-mannered young men, Gonzalez became characterized as a rebel from a poor Mexican-American family. Some writers called him "the kid from the other side of the tracks." Gonzalez felt that this description was an exaggeration of the working-class home in which he grew up.[4] But the image stuck and many people found it fascinating.

In addition, Gonzalez had a tremendous charisma that drew people to him. He was confident and easygoing on the court. He was also handsome. Writers noted that groups of young ladies often came to watch him play.

Fans also found Gonzalez's heritage intriguing. He was the first person of color to win the national title. Some reporters emphasized his Mexican background by calling him Pancho, Chuck Pate's nickname for his friend. But the name felt different coming from the press, and Gonzalez hated it.[5]

Pancho was a name some people used to address Mexican-American males without bothering to learn their names. It was sometimes intended to refer to a person of low social status. Many Mexican-Americans, in fact, considered the nickname to be a racial slur. It reminded them of the negative stereotype some people had about them. This stereotype unfairly portrayed Mexicans as stupid and lazy.

Indeed, writers continued reporting that Gonzalez had a lackadaisical approach to life and tennis. One wrote, "Next to eating Mexican food, the thing California-born Richard A. [Gonzalez]

Richard was very popular with the ladies.

probably enjoys more than anything else is taking life easy. When the mood hits him, 'Pancho' plays tennis."[6]

While the press called Gonzalez "Pancho," the people closest to him respected his wishes and called him Richard. No matter what people called him, though, people did call him. He was suddenly in demand for radio, newspaper, and magazine interviews. His social calendar filled with parties and dinners in his honor. He was a frequent guest of wealthy tennis fans.

Gonzalez was completely at home on the tennis court. But the off-court world of championship tennis was not as comfortable. This was a world of the rich and the privileged. Most tennis stars were at ease in this environment. Gonzalez was not. His working-class background had given him no exposure to this world. He was keenly aware of this and felt out of place at many tennis functions. He much preferred the company of his old friends at Exposition Park.[7]

Richard (third from the left) preferred the company of his friends back home.

In fact, Gonzalez still frequented Exposition Park and played tennis with his friends there. Some people commented that this habit would ruin Gonzalez's game.

He felt differently. Exposition Park was a unique environment at the time. Many talented players, including those of color, congregated there.

Two of the most well known were Jimmy McDaniels and Oscar Johnson. In 1940, McDaniels had been the Negro National Champion. As for Johnson, he had recently won the National Public Parks Championship in the eighteen-and-under division.

Consequently, competition and expertise at Exposition Park were plentiful. Gonzalez knew his game would not suffer from play there. More bothersome to him were the comments that questioned his status as the top U.S. player.

Many people did not see him as a true champion. They believed that if Schroeder had entered the 1948 U.S. National Championships, he would have beaten Gonzalez. Therefore Gonzalez felt he had something to prove when he met Schroeder in the Pacific Southwest Tournament that fall.

Gonzalez stepped up to the task in front of a capacity crowd at the Los Angeles Tennis Club and failed. Schroeder beat him in the tournament's semifinals. In Gonzalez's words, Schroeder "showed no respect at all for the new crown that had been placed on my head."[8]

There would soon be a new joy in Gonzalez's life, though. In December, Henrietta gave birth to a baby boy. The Gonzalezes named their new son Richard Alonzo, Jr. Now, between fatherhood and socializing, Gonzalez found little time for training. By the end of the month he had gained twenty-five pounds. The extra weight hurt his tennis game.

In February, both Gonzalez and Schroeder entered another California tournament. Gonzalez looked forward to another chance to prove he deserved the national title. Then, the day before he was to play Schroeder in the final match, Gonzalez's partner in a doubles match accidentally smashed him in the face with his racket. The blow broke Gonzalez's nose.

Nevertheless, Gonzalez was determined to keep his appointment with Schroeder. The next day he arrived at the court with a bandaged nose. Although he had to breathe out of his mouth, he managed to beat Schroeder 6–2, 6–8, 9–7. Gonzalez later said he would happily break his nose every day of the week if it meant playing that well.[9]

In May, Gonzalez faced Schroeder again in the Southern California Championships. This time Schroeder won in less than forty minutes. One observer noted that the contest was over before Gonzalez had even warmed up. Four days later, Gonzalez played

Ted Schroeder, Herb Flam, Gene Garrett, Pancho Gonzalez, and William S. Kellogg at the La Jolla Beach and Tennis Club.

in the French National Championships at Paris where he lost to another American, Budge Patty.

By June, Gonzalez was again feeling a need to prove himself worthy of the U.S. Championship. Wimbledon loomed ahead, the most important amateur tennis tournament of all. Even so, Gonzalez turned down offers of instruction from the best coaches around, people who might have helped him gain consistency in his shot-making. "My game has to be careless," Gonzalez said, defending his decision. "That's the way it's built."[10]

But the tension was mounting. Schroeder and other world-class players would be at Wimbledon. Even Gonzalez's mother noticed an uncharacteristic seriousness in her son as the tournament approached. "Something is happening to Richard," she said. "When he [had] his picture taken for the passport, I [asked] the photographer to take four extra pictures. In only one picture was he smiling. He is not so happy any more playing tennis. I do not like that."[11]

One writer put it another way, "Gonzalez knows he must win at Wimbledon, and the knowledge is forcing him, somewhat against his will, to grow up."[12]

In late June 1949, Richard Gonzalez walked onto a Wimbledon court for the first time in his life. In light of his numerous losses that year, the reigning U.S. Champion was only seeded second. Schroeder was honored with the number-one spot. This seeding predicted a final match between Gonzalez and Schroeder. But Gonzalez never made it past the third round of play. He was eliminated by Australian Geoff Brown. Schroeder, on the other hand, battled his way to the final where he beat Drobny for the Wimbledon title. Gonzalez did get a measure of revenge when he and Parker beat Schroeder and Mulloy for that year's Wimbledon doubles title.

Still, some felt that because of his erratic record Gonzalez should not be placed on the 1949 Davis Cup Team. This would have left him deeply disappointed, as playing for the U.S. was one of Gonzalez's greatest desires.

When he learned he had made the team, Gonzalez was determined to show he deserved the honor. He defeated two Australians—Frank Sedgman and Billy Sidwell—to earn two of the three points the U.S. needed to win the three out of five match competition. By earning two points by himself, Gonzalez was an essential member of that year's U.S. Davis Cup team. The wins also boosted Gonzalez's morale, and he felt ready to win the U.S. National Championship.[13]

Others were not as confident. After reviewing his record, more and more tennis fans seemed to believe that Gonzalez's 1948 victory had been a combination of luck and Schroeder's absence from the tournament. Because of this, one sportswriter called Gonzalez the greatest "cheese champion" in tennis history, meaning that Gonzalez had won the U.S. title in a cheesy or cheap way.[14] Now Gonzalez was dubbed with another nickname some say he detested—"Gorgo," short for Gorgonzola cheese.

Experts felt that the U.S. Championships final match would be another Gonzalez-Schroeder showdown. Most favored Schroeder. However, these forecasters did not know how much being called the "cheese champion" hurt Gonzalez. Nor did they know how determined this made him.

Something else motivated Gonzalez. A man named Bobby Riggs was looking for new talent. Riggs was the promoter of the most prominent professional tennis tour in the world. Every year he hired a few of the best players to compete against each other in cities all over the globe. At the time, Riggs was looking for someone to challenge his latest star, Jack Kramer. Many people assumed that Riggs would ask the winner of the 1949 U.S. National Championships to turn professional. Riggs's touring contract could be worth as much as $75,000. This thought energized Gonzalez.[15]

Being a top-ranked amateur was a career that needed full-time attention. It meant hours of daily training and frequent trips away from home for tournaments. These commitments made it almost impossible for a serious amateur to hold a regular job. Most amateurs, therefore, had to rely on other sources of income to pay their living expenses.

Gonzalez had no other sources of income. "As an amateur," he later reported, "I saved enough from the expense money I received to be able to practice and play occasionally in the off season... I just managed to get by when I was out of competition, but I had to scrape."[16]

In addition, Gonzalez now had a family to support. Earning money was a necessity, and doing it by playing professional tennis would be a dream come true.

At Forest Hills the tournament officials seeded Schroeder first and Gonzalez second. Both men won their early rounds of play and advanced to the final. As Gonzalez readied himself for the 1949 championship match, he knew he was playing for more than a title—he was playing for a dream.

1 "Mañana Comes," *Time*, May 19, 1947, p.50.
2 *Current Biography Yearbook,* 1949 (New York: H. W. Wilson, 1949), p.231.
3 "Indoors and Out," *Time*, April 4, 1949, p.77.
4 Cy Rice, *Man With a Racket: The Autobiography of Pancho Gonzales* (New York: A. S. Barnes and Company, 1959), p.63.
5 John Sharnik, *Remembrance of Games Past* (New York: MacMillan Publishing Company, 1986), p.255.
6 "Indoors and Out," p.77.
7 Rice, p. 87.
8 Ibid., p.81.
9 Ibid., p.83.
10 Gene Farmer, "Pancho Gonzalez," *Life*, June 6, 1949, p.68.
11 Ibid., p.72.
12 Ibid.
13 Rice, p.84.
14 Farmer, p.67.
15 Allison Danzig, "Anyone for Tennis? Yes, Gonzalez," *New York Times Magazine*, May 1957, p.42.
16 Ibid.

The Way Up

It took a record-breaking thirty-four games for Schroeder to beat Gonzalez in the first set. Yet Gonzalez was not about to give up. As the match wore on, he battled for every point. The crowd sensed his determination. Many found their admiration for him growing with every grueling point he won.

By the fifth and final set, spectators were cheering for Gonzalez. They were impressed with his lightning serve and powerful shots. More than anything, though, they were awed by his resolve to win. It had been three hours since the contest began, and every point had been hard-won.

Finally, the match seemed near an end. Gonzalez had broken Schroeder's serve, and Schroeder seemed to be weakening as Gonzalez continued his attack. Gonzalez went up by one point, and the crowd sat riveted by the action.

Then came a drive down the sideline from Schroeder that Gonzalez did not return. Time stood still while everyone awaited the linesman's call. When he signaled out-of-bounds, the crowd went wild! Richard Gonzalez was the 1949 United States tennis champion!

Allison Danzig reported in the next day's *New York Times* that Gonzalez had shown outstanding perseverance, moral fiber, and good sportsmanship.[1] As for Gonzalez, he was just happy to shed the nickname "cheese champion." He later reported that the best part of winning was appearing on the cover of a magazine called *American Lawn Tennis.*[2] Appropriately, the caption read "The Last Laugh."

On September 20, 1949, Gonzalez turned professional. He signed a contract to become part of Bobby Riggs's 1950 tennis tour. Gonzalez would play a series of matches against Jack Kramer for a guaranteed salary of $60,000. The winner of the most matches at the end of the tour would be considered the world professional champion.

Most experts felt that Gonzalez was too inexperienced to turn professional. But financial realities made the move logical to Gonzalez. Henrietta was about to have their second son, Michael. Soon Gonzalez would have two children and a wife to support. Besides, Gonzalez was full of optimism and confidence. So he packed his bags and bade his family good-bye.

Now several nights each week Gonzalez laced up his shoes to face Jack Kramer. Although his opponent never changed, the city where they played always did. From Boston to Chicago to Memphis, Tennessee, Gonzalez and Kramer traversed the U.S. by car. At each destination they played a three-set match, often on a canvas court that traveled with them.

Life on the professional tennis tour was demanding.[3] No matter how Gonzalez felt, the match always went on. One night he told his opponent that he had sprained an ankle and could not play. "What do you mean—can't play?" Kramer asked him. "We always play."[4] So Gonzalez received a shot of Novocain for his pain and hit the court.

After beating Schroeder, Gonzalez had the last laugh.

The inexperienced Gonzalez challenges professional champion Jack Kramer.

Gonzalez learned quickly that Kramer was a merciless opponent. He never let up even when he was several points ahead. Gonzalez later said that Kramer was one of the toughest competitors he had ever faced.

Yet this did not discourage Gonzalez. In fact, the high level of competition inspired him. Most notably, he saw the value of Kramer's killer instinct and further developed his own. Gonzalez once observed, "Most [players] would crush their poor old mothers, 6–0, if she stood in the path of a championship."[5]

Kramer used winning tactics off the court too. For example, knowing that Gonzalez loved soft drinks, he arranged to have ice-cold sodas placed on the side of the court at all of their matches. Kramer was not being kind, though. He believed that soft drinks were unhealthy and would weaken an athlete. By providing Gonzalez with them, he hoped to gain a slight edge over him.[6]

Kramer, however, did not need any extra advantages. He trounced Gonzalez night after night. Each loss was painful to Gonzalez because it represented a threat to his livelihood. The winning player on this tour would be asked back the next year. The loser had no such guarantee. By the tour's end, Kramer had beaten Gonzalez ninety-six matches to twenty-seven. This confirmed the belief of many that he had turned professional too soon. Even so, Gonzalez had made more than $70,000, a tremendous amount of money in 1950.

Money, however, could not mend Gonzalez's broken ego. Nor could it guarantee Gonzalez a future in professional tennis. A grim Gonzalez headed back to Los Angeles, hoping that Riggs would find a place for him on the 1951 tour. But Riggs did not.

Richard Gonzalez was only twenty-one years old when Bobby Riggs told him he was "past tense." As Riggs so bluntly put it, "You came, you saw—and Jack Kramer conquered."[7]

Then Riggs offered Gonzalez the faintest glimmer of hope. He advised Gonzalez to stay in shape and play in all the professional tournaments he could. If he proved he was still a top competitor, he might get another chance on a future tour.

On his first professional tennis tour, Gonzalez faced Jack Kramer in 123 matches. Gonzalez lost all but twenty-seven of them.

Soon the next year's touring players were announced. The invincible Jack Kramer would meet Francisco Segura, a player from Ecuador. Segura was called Pancho, too. However, "Pancho" is a common nickname for Francisco. So in Segura's case, the nickname "Pancho" did not carry the same negative connotation it did with Gonzalez.

Segura, like Gonzalez, had an unusual background for a tennis player of the time. He had grown up in a cane shack on the grounds of a tennis club where his father was the groundskeeper. He had been struck by rickets when he was a child. Rickets is a disease that makes the bones soft and weak. But Segura was strong-willed and driven to play tennis. He learned to swing the racket with both hands for more strength. His two-handed forehand is considered to be one of the greatest strokes in tennis history. This, plus his fast nimble footwork, made him a top competitor. Gonzalez and Segura became close friends on tour and remained so throughout their lives.

Now, as Kramer and Segura headed off to play tennis, Gonzalez stayed home playing at Exposition Park. Gonzalez missed the intensity of constant competition. To stay active, he took up golf. It bored him.

Next he tried gambling. Night after night Gonzalez drove to poker parlors outside of Los Angeles where he matched wits with experienced gamblers. The high stakes for which they played provided the

Bill Bond, Sr., Pancho Segura, Bobby Riggs, Pancho Gonzalez and Jack Kramer at the La Jolla Beach and Tennis Club.

excitement Gonzalez craved. Unfortunately, he often lost. Before long finances forced him to find a different hobby.

Gonzalez turned to car racing. Henrietta objected to her husband's latest pastime because of its danger. She urged him to think of his family. With the birth of another child, Danny, Gonzalez now had three sons. But Gonzalez told his wife that the excitement was just what he needed to take his mind off of professional tennis. Car racing would become a lifelong love for Gonzalez.

Racing was not the only thing that Gonzalez and Henrietta argued about. While his tennis career collapsed, Gonzalez's marriage was deteriorating, also. Gonzalez moved out of his house in March 1952. For the next three years he would live in a series of apartments, saying that home was wherever he kept his tennis rackets.

**The Gonzalez Family: Richard, Henrietta, Richard Jr.,
Danny (center) and Michael.**

When the Olympic Tennis Shop was put up for sale, it seemed natural for Gonzalez to buy it. For several months he operated the little store. He also trained hard during this time, working to improve his game. Much of his training was done at Exposition Park. He often played with Oscar Johnson who gave Gonzalez a good workout.

Big Pancho Gonzalez and little Pancho Segura at the Beverly Wilshire Hotel. Actor Walter Pidgeon is seated in the umpire's chair.

Occasionally Gonzalez also played at the Los Angeles Tennis Club. Remembering Riggs's advice, Gonzalez entered whatever professional tournaments he could. The most important of these was the U.S. Professional Championships. For a time, this tournament was called the World Professional Tennis Championships.

In 1952, Gonzalez made it to the final round of this tournament where he faced Kramer's latest vanquished opponent, Francisco Segura. Segura beat Gonzalez, but the match was very close.

Gonzalez (right) proved he had become the best player in the world by winning the 1953 World's Professional Tennis Championship.

Gonzalez did win four tournaments that year. In these he was beating all the top players consistently, including Kramer. Many people believed he was now the best player in the world.

Gonzalez was back at the World Professional Tennis Championships in 1953. This time he won the tournament by beating Don Budge, the former winner of the Grand Slam. By now Bobby Riggs had retired as promoter of the professional tennis tour and Jack Kramer had become the new promoter.

In 1954, Kramer retired from actually competing on the tour. His retirement made way for a new professional tennis champion. As the newest promoter, Kramer promptly offered contracts to four of the men he thought most capable of filling his shoes: Francisco "Pancho" Segura, Frank Sedgman, Don Budge, and Richard Gonzalez. Now, three years after his devastating debut on the professional tour, Gonzalez was back.

Kramer's 1954 tour would be different from the previous head-to-head tours between the reigning professional king and the newly turned-pro amateur champion. Instead, this tour would be a round robin contest in which four players continually played each other. The two winners of one night's two matches would play each other the following night. Likewise, the losers would face off. The man who had won the most matches at the end of the tour would be declared the new professional tennis champion. Although each player received the same pay whether he won or lost, Gonzalez knew that for him, especially, the stakes for winning this tour were enormous. Losing again might bring a permanent end to his tennis career.

Each of the four men on the tour was able and fierce. But Gonzalez beat them all. As if to emphasize his worthiness, he also won the 1954 World Professional Tennis Championship.

Gonzalez moved back home in March 1955. He and Henrietta decided to give their marriage another chance. He was thrilled with the reconciliation and glad to be living with his sons again. Richard Jr., helped his father tinker with his racecars. He also played tennis with him, and Gonzalez claimed his son already showed talent.

In 1955, Gonzalez won the World Professional Tennis Championship once more. Spalding Sports Company had already begun selling a tennis racket named after and signed by Gonzalez. This marked the beginning of a long business relationship; Gonzalez would help design and sign Spalding rackets for the next twenty-five years.

At the time, Tony Trabert ruled the amateur tennis world. Trabert had won three of the four major national championships in 1955—those of France, Great Britain (Wimbledon), and the U.S. Soon after winning the U.S. title, Trabert turned professional. He signed a contract with Kramer to play in a 1955–1956 tour.

Kramer considered coming out of retirement to oppose Trabert. However, Gonzalez's wife Henrietta went to Kramer. She convinced him that Gonzalez should play the tour since he was clearly the best player in the world. Kramer agreed that there was only one person capable of giving Trabert any real competition—Pancho Gonzalez. So Kramer offered Gonzalez a chance to tour against Trabert.

Gonzalez was happy to be on another tour. But its financial arrangements angered him. Trabert was guaranteed earnings of $75,000. Gonzalez, however, was promised only $15,000.[8] This seemed terribly unfair, and Gonzalez looked for an explanation.

According to Kramer, the salary difference was because Gonzalez was a risk. Kramer claimed arena owners were not sure Gonzalez would draw an audience. They worried that fans would remember how badly Kramer had beaten Gonzalez on the 1949–1950 tour and would not come to see him play Trabert. If no one came to the matches, the tour would not make money.

Richard Gonzalez's name was synonymous with championship tennis. For many years, Spalding Sports manufactured a "Pancho Gonzales" signature racket with a color picture of Richard's face.

Some people did not think this was the reason for the pay discrepancy. They believed that Kramer had to pay Trabert the large sum to lure him from amateur status. On the other hand, Kramer knew that Gonzalez would play for the lower sum just to get back on the tour.

Frustrated, Gonzalez trained harder than ever. He lost weight and sharpened his volley. He improved his already powerful serve. When he saw Trabert he told him, "You'd better get used to losing."[9] Trabert had little choice.

By March, Gonzalez was leading Trabert thirty-four matches to eleven. When the tour ended, Gonzalez had conquered Trabert seventy-four matches to twenty-four. The lopsided record was proof of Gonzalez's amazing play. It was also evidence of how Gonzalez handled his resentment for the unequal pay—on the court. He was a relentless opponent who never let up, no matter what the score.

During the tour, Gonzalez and Trabert had often traded insults on and off the court. This resulted in a lifelong dislike between the two men. Even so, after the tour Trabert praised Gonzalez's tennis. "Gonzalez is the greatest natural athlete tennis has ever known," he said. "The way he can move that 6-foot 3-inch frame of his around the court is almost unbelievable...He instinctively does the right thing at the right time. Doesn't even have to stop to think."[10]

In 1956, Gonzalez won the World Professional Tennis Championship for the fourth straight year. He also won the prestigious London Professional Championship at Wembley, England for the fourth time. The final match against Frank Sedgman lasted so long that all forms of public transportation had stopped running long before it ended. Yet the spectators stayed, entranced with Gonzalez's dynamic and explosive tennis. His serve continued to be his greatest strength, and it was once clocked at 120 miles per hour. This was the fastest serve among the professionals.

Gonzalez's opponent for the 1957 tour was an Australian named Ken Rosewall. Rosewall was an Australian, French, and U.S. singles champion. Gonzalez won the opening match of the tour, then kept on winning. By the time the two had played sixty matches, Gonzalez had won forty of them.

**Gonzalez hits a backhand lob behind his back
while playing against Ken Rosewall.**

In fact, Gonzalez was so good that some fans seemed bored with the tour. Fearing that a loss of interest would mean a loss in profit, Kramer asked Gonzalez to take it easy on Rosewall. Although Kramer did not want Gonzalez to actually lose matches on purpose, he asked Gonzalez to let Rosewall stay close enough to maintain a little excitement. Reluctantly, Gonzalez agreed.

Shortly after their talk, though, Gonzalez told Kramer that giving up points was ruining his concentration. Kramer understood and realized that his request had been unreasonable. He told Gonzalez to forget their deal.

When the Gonzalez-Rosewall tour ended, Gonzalez had beaten Rosewall fifty matches to twenty-six. Gonzalez was clearly the new king of professional tennis. As one writer put it, Gonzalez had "emerged from the bloody free-for-all with Jack Kramer's abandoned crown clenched in his predatory jaws."[11]

---

1 Allison Danzig, "Champion Rallies To Score in 5 Sets," *The New York Times,* September 6, 1949, p.33.
2 Himilce Novas, *The Hispanic 100: A Ranking of the Latino Men and Women Who Have Most Influenced American Thought and Culture* (New York: A Citadel Press Book, 1995), p.232.
3 Andrea Leand, "The Lone Wolf," *Tennis Week,* July 20, 1995, p.13.
4 Bud Collins, *My Life With the Pros* (New York: E.P. Dutton, 1989), p.127.
5 Cy Rice, *Man With a Racket: The Autobiography of Pancho Gonzales* (New York: A. S. Barnes and Company, 1959), p.157.
6 John Sharnik, *Remembrance of Games Past* (New York: MacMillan Publishing Company, 1986), p.254.
7 Rice, p.101.
8 "Pancho At 41," *Time,* February 16, 1970, p.57.
9 Ibid.
10 Rice, p.129.
11 Sharnik., p.255.

Fifty Points on Terror

By now, Richard Gonzalez was known everywhere as the best tennis player in the world. In addition to his reputation for great tennis, he had developed a reputation for his personality. When Gonzalez first stepped into the public spotlight, he had been described as charismatic and confident. But as the years progressed, some people came to see this self-assurance as conceit.

These people's opinion was not improved by Gonzalez's curt treatment of his fans. He regularly refused to sign autographs before matches, making some of them feel he was mean-spirited and haughty. Gonzalez defended his actions by saying that he had to conserve his energy for competition. Besides, he said, he was usually preoccupied with tactical thoughts before his matches. But Gonzalez did sign autographs after many matches—especially victorious ones.

Gonzalez was also criticized for the outspoken manner in which he questioned line-calls with which he disagreed. He became known for the icy glares and sarcastic remarks he directed at officials. For example, after a call went against him, he would turn to the crowd and ask, "Is there an eye doctor about?"[1]

Many incidents were more confrontational. During one match, Gonzalez became particularly short-tempered as a heckler shouted at him. After several catcalls, Gonzalez demanded that the heckler show his face. He did not. Then, as Gonzalez prepared to serve a game-winning point, the heckler shouted again to distract him. Gonzalez stopped for a moment to regain his concentration. When he served, he double-faulted and went on to lose the game. While walking to the other side of the court, Gonzalez took an angry swing at a microphone standing next to the court and sent it flying.[2]

On another occasion Gonzalez was in a rage over the loud noise made by a clock. To quiet it, he smashed a ball into the glass clock face, completely shattering it. Later, Gonzalez paid to have it repaired.

Another time Gonzalez was battling Rosewall in a match that seemed to last forever. One sports reporter worried that he would not make his deadline if he waited until the end of the match to start writing his story. So he pulled out his portable typewriter and began typing. A few other reporters did the same. The tap-tap-tapping of the typewriters began to annoy Gonzalez.

He shouted up at the reporters to quiet down. Assuming that Gonzalez was complaining about a situation on the court, the writers ignored him. So Gonzalez started slamming balls into the press section.

According to one of the reporters, "I was just working, not paying attention to [Gonzalez's] yelling, until a ball parted my hair and crashed behind me. It was like a rocket attack, and we were, literally, sitting ducks in the front row upstairs. Pancho scared the hell out of us. I've ducked foul balls in the press box at Fenway Park, but they come one at a time, and the batter isn't aiming at you. Pancho was out to get us, hitting balls as fast and hard as he could. They were smashing all around us."[3]

Newspapers and magazines regularly reported Gonzalez's outbursts. His talent for terrorizing locker rooms became well known.

Gonzalez was known to have disagreements with tennis officials. Here he is shown with Jimmy Van Alen of the Newport Casino, who first used the tie-break, in a tournament he ran there.

One writer recalled a time when Gonzalez was angry with courtside photographers because their flashbulbs kept distracting him during his match. Afterward, Gonzalez stormed into the locker room shouting and throwing rackets. One player hid behind a shower curtain during the tirade while another ducked under a table.[4]

Some people believed Gonzalez's manners were proof of his low social status. But many enjoyed his antics. Over time, he developed a large following of admirers. They saw his passion for every point as evidence of a highly competitive spirit. There was a purity about Gonzalez. He did not want popularity or acclaim. He simply wanted to play tennis.

And he charmed many of the people who came to watch him play—even those who had previously thought him obnoxious. There was something undeniably alluring about the handsome man who played ferocious tennis. As one writer put it, Gonzalez brought "more magnetism onto a tennis court than anyone who ever played the game."[5]

He also brought more emotion. Gonzalez knew that his court etiquette was less than perfect. But he maintained that most of his poor manners were caused by frustration at himself for making mistakes. In addition, the world of professional tennis was often brutal. It was a business to the promoters and a job for Gonzalez—a job he would lose if his tennis was not up to par.

Gonzalez believed that under these circumstances, showing one's emotions was natural and healthy. "For players under pressure," he said, "emotion is a way of stimulating yourself. In tennis, there is no [other] way to do it, and it's unfair to ask a player to hold it in."[6]

But Gonzalez's opponents were not always sure he was simply giving himself a pep talk. Rosewall, for instance, said that Gonzalez's whole demeanor on the court exuded a "general air of violence."[7]

Some people claimed that Gonzalez used his size and fireworks to intimidate opponents and referees. Rosewall himself admitted that he had to be careful not to let Gonzalez ruin his concentration. As Kramer put it, "Pancho gets 50 points on his serve and 50 points on terror."[8]

Those closest to Gonzalez knew that his explosive nature was caused by something besides trying to win tennis matches. They knew his attitude was partially caused by an inner rage. Some of this rage came from Gonzalez's awareness that many people in the elite circle of championship tennis thought of him as inferior. Gonzalez avoided these people as much as possible.

While at home, Gonzalez preferred the company of family and close friends. And though he could also be temperamental with

Gonzalez was on Jack Kramer's pro tour for many years. Today, Kramer's tour truck can be seen at the International Tennis Hall of Fame in Newport, Rhode Island.

them, those who knew him best described him as honest and considerate. Among them, Gonzalez was known for unusual acts of kindness.

When Gonzalez was on a tennis tour, he spent most of his time alone. He ate by himself and spent his days in his hotel room reading about cars. Sometimes he took a drive into the surrounding countryside.

At times one of his brothers, usually Ralph, accompanied him. More often Gonzalez traveled alone, driving from stop to stop in his own sports car while his fellow competitors shared rides together. Because of this Gonzalez earned another nickname—"The Lone Wolf."

But though Gonzalez claimed to prefer solitude, it sometimes had its drawbacks. "Because when you lose you are down," he said, "depressed and thousands of miles away from home which depresses you more, and tears come to your eyes. And you are all alone."[9]

Gonzalez found another disadvantage to the traveling lifestyle. Occasionally, he was the victim of prejudice. One blatant incident happened in the 1950s when he, his brother Manuel, and Segura were traveling on tour together.

They entered a Texas cafe, none of them noticing a sign hanging near the door that said, "No Mexicans served here." They sat down, and no one waited on them. When Gonzalez learned why, he felt as if he would explode. But then he remembered his grandmother's advice and imagined the owner of the cafe in his underwear. The ridiculous idea didn't help his anger to fade. The hurt from the incident would last for some time.[10]

When Gonzalez returned to Los Angeles after this tour, he talked with other Mexican-Americans about racism. He learned that discrimination was a negative force in many of their lives. Gonzalez was moved by their pain and wished he could do something about it.

Actually, his presence in professional tennis was doing more for oppressed people than he may have known. Richard Gonzalez was one of the few Latinos many people in the U.S. had ever encountered, even if it was only through the sports pages of the newspaper. He made them aware that many Latinos had been born and raised in the U.S. and were citizens just like themselves.

Other Latinos took pride in Gonzalez's achievements. His success in the upper-class world of tennis inspired them. Some took up tennis themselves. Others gained strength from his example and faced racism with more resolve.

Furthermore, Gonzalez served as an inspiration to working-class people from all ethnic backgrounds. He was an underdog, a solitary rebel. His life revolved around one goal—playing excellent tennis.

While on tour, Gonzalez receives the city key in Juarez, Mexico.

Even those who did not like tennis could identify with Gonzalez's struggle in an unfriendly world. Many of them also struggled to achieve a dream.

Yet sometimes it seemed to Gonzalez that his battles would never end. Throughout his years on the professional tour, he and Jack Kramer had feuded constantly over Gonzalez's salary. Gonzalez felt that Kramer was exploiting him. He believed he deserved a larger share of the tour's profits since no one could beat him more than occasionally.[11] Gonzalez's outstanding play was a powerful drawing card for audiences. So were his charismatic presence and his unpredictable conduct. He created such great drama and excitement that people realized they were experiencing something phenomenal. Gonzalez often played to sold-out audiences.

When Kramer refused to increase Gonzalez's salary, Gonzalez made his complaints public. He told a reporter from *The New York Times* that he was considering breaking his contract with Kramer. Gonzalez went on to say, "I think I am entitled to the top position in pro tennis and that my record against Tony Trabert and Ken Rosewall and against other players in tournaments proves it."[12]

But Kramer refused to change the terms of their contract. This left Gonzalez legally tied to Kramer through 1960 or until he lost a tour title. This did not look like it was going to happen any time soon.

In the meantime, Gonzalez continued working on his game. As he had in his youth, he watched others to see what he could learn from them. Sometimes he copied a training method or figured out a new kind of shot. He practiced six hours a day on the court, then did off-court conditioning as well.

As for Kramer, he, too, was tired of fighting over Gonzalez's salary. So he searched for someone who could beat him. He recruited the 1956 and 1957 Wimbledon champion, Lew Hoad. Kramer thought this Australian just might unseat Gonzalez. Hoad was a powerful hitter who had also won the Australian and French titles in 1956. "If Hoad could beat [Gonzalez] that was my chance to get rid of that tiger," Kramer remarked, adding, "[Gonzalez] knew what I was doing, too, and he was furious."[13]

Now Kramer did something he had never done before. He helped one of the competitors. Kramer took Hoad on a tour of Europe, Africa, India, and Southeast Asia to get him in shape for his head-to-head tour with Gonzalez. In effect, Kramer became Hoad's personal coach. Both Hoad and Gonzalez were physically powerful, aggressive hitters, and strikingly good-looking.

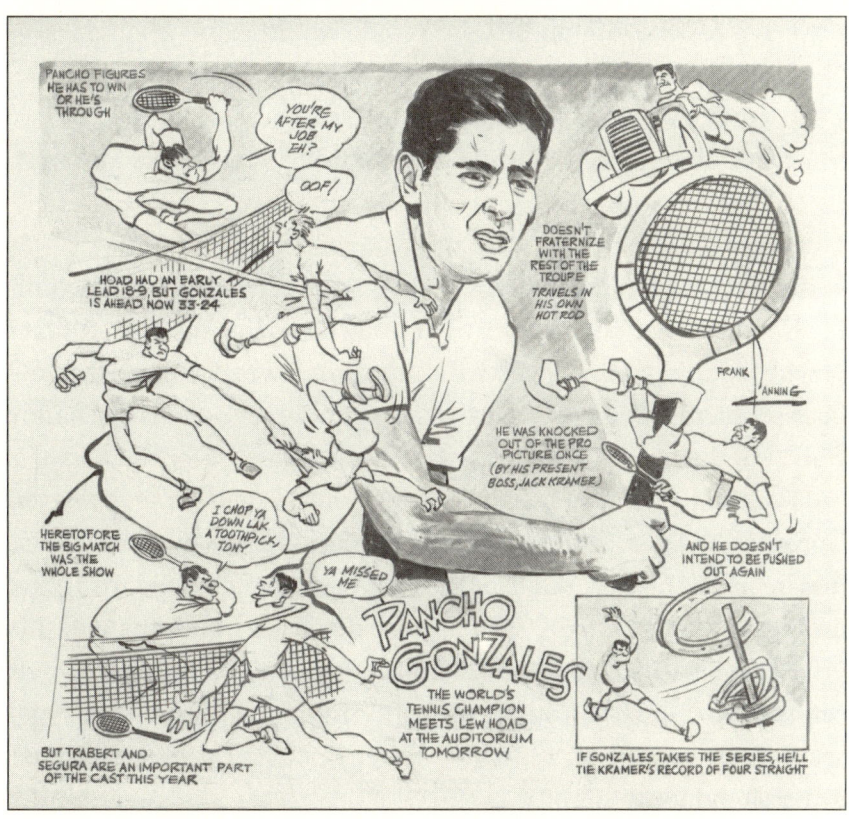

A newspaper cartoon during the Gonzalez-Hoad tour.

The Gonzalez-Hoad tour began in Australia in January 1958. It soon looked like Hoad just might knock Gonzalez out of the top spot. The two played great tennis and neither man was willing to yield an inch on the court. Many contests went to five sets, and some of these lasted for hours.

Some consider these matches to be the greatest tennis ever played. One observer noted,

> "Both guys were such great players with big serves. Gonzalez would hit that serve, and Hoad would return it like a ping-pong ball. They would go corner to corner. Boom! Boom! BOOM! People would stand up and applaud, thinking the point was over, and it would keep going two or three more shots. Or two or three more exchanges. People would be screaming. I tell you, man, that was tennis!"[14]

When the tour ended its Australian segment, Gonzalez was trailing Hoad by five matches. But then Hoad began losing. The strain of playing against Gonzalez with his unusual power had caused an old back problem to flare up. There were nights when Hoad could barely walk, but the tennis matches always went on.

Eventually, Hoad's back improved. In the meantime, however, Gonzalez had been able to correct a weakness in his own play. Hoad had been taking advantage of the way Gonzalez gripped his racket on his backhand stroke. Gonzalez realized this and changed his grip. This gave him more power and versatility.[15] By the end of their series, Gonzalez had caught up with and passed Hoad. The final series score was 51 to 36 matches. Gonzalez had won yet another professional tour!

Gonzalez begins to turn the tide on Hoad. Here they are competing at the Los Angeles Tennis Club.

Curiously, though, Hoad had made $148,000 on the tour while Gonzalez went home with only $100,000.[16]

When Gonzalez faced Hoad in the final of the 1958 World Professional Tennis Championships, he was victorious again. Now the winner of the most important professional tour had also won the most important professional tournament for the sixth time. Gonzalez remained the master of tennis at its highest level.

Gonzalez thrived in this world. He once said,

"The hardest part of it is when you lay off and have to work to keep in condition. While on tour I don't regard it as work. I can't go to the movies or watch television as often as I would like because of the eye strain. There are eight hours during the day when you have nothing to do, lying around for the match in the evening. It can get boring. But once I'm on the court I'm doing the thing I want to do, and I am very happy with my life."[17]

1 "Best In the World," *Time*, February 11, 1957, p.59.
2 Cy Rice, *Man With a Racket: The Autobiography of Pancho Gonzales* (New York: A. S. Barnes and Company, 1959), pp.179–180.
3 Bud Collins, *My Life With the Pros* (New York: E.P. Dutton, 1989), p.88.
4 Richard Evans, *Open Tennis* (London: Bloomsbury, 1988), p.3.
5 "Pancho Turns Them On," *Newsweek*, September 16, 1968, p.62.
6 Richard "Pancho"Gonzalez, "Freedom of Choice and the Davis Cup," *World Tennis*, August 1985, p.80.
7 John Sharnik, *Remembrance of Games Past* (New York: MacMillan Publishing Company, 1986), pp.255–256.
8 "Pancho at 41," *Time*, February 16, 1970, p.57.
9 Andrea Leand, "The Lone Wolf," *Tennis Week*, July 20, 1995, pp.13 & 34.
10 Rice, pp.134–135.
11 Allison Danzig, "Anyone for Tennis? Yes, Gonzalez," *New York Times Magazine*, May 1957, p.42.
12 Ibid., p.44.
13 Bud Collins and Zander Hollander, *Bud Collins' Modern Encyclopedia of Tennis* (New York: Doubleday and Company, 1980), pp.107–108.
14 Sharnik, p.257.
15 Trent Frayne, *Famous Tennis Players* (United States: PMA Communications, Incorporated, 1977), p.115.
16 Collins and Hollander, p.111.
17 Danzig, p.14.

Transitions

Professional tennis kept Gonzalez on the road much of the time. When he was at home, he enjoyed pool, poker, bowling, and hunting. He also still liked car racing.

In fact, he and his brother Ralph had formed a drag-racing team called the Gonzales Brothers. Richard tuned the dragster and Ralph drove it. The Gonzales Brothers was one of the top teams around. They qualified second at the 1958 U.S. Nationals and even broke a few speed records.

Henrietta was not impressed. Gonzalez was in perpetual motion, and she wanted him to spend more time with his family. Although Gonzalez said that he loved his wife, he knew he could not be the kind of husband she wanted.[1] In December of 1958 the two were divorced.

In the meantime, Gonzalez worked with a writer named Cy Rice preparing his autobiography. The book was called *Man With a Racket* and it was published in 1959. Francisco Segura wrote the

Ralph drives the Gonzales Brothers dragster to three straight wins at San Fernando drag strip.

book's introduction, noting that Gonzalez was like a hurricane with one exception. As Segura put it, "Weather is fairly predictable."[2]

In many ways, though, Gonzalez was entirely predictable. While on a tour, he focused solely on his tennis and preferred to be left alone. His powerful serve remained his biggest asset, and some people believe it is what made him the world's best player. Gonzalez himself did not think his serve was any better than it had been during his amateur days. But, he said, his volley and ground strokes were definitely stronger. Most importantly, he noted, they were more consistent.

In 1959, Kramer promoted a round-robin tour. This time Gonzalez would compete against Hoad, Mal Anderson, and Ashley

Cooper. The newest professionals, Anderson and Cooper, were both fierce opponents. Cooper, in fact, had won three of the four Grand Slam tournaments of 1958. Yet Gonzalez beat them all. He then went on to defeat Hoad 6–4, 6–2, 6–4 in the final of the World Professional Tennis Championship for a seventh tournament title.

Even so, a friendship had developed between Hoad and Gonzalez and they admired each other's tennis skills. Gonzalez often said that when Lew Hoad was at his peak, nobody could touch him. As for Hoad, he often described Gonzalez as the greatest tennis player ever.

On the basis of his record, Gonzalez tried to renegotiate his contract with Kramer once more. This time he gave Kramer an ultimatum. Until their differences were settled, Gonzalez refused to go out on tour. He told one reporter, "Kramer needs me and I need Jack. He is the promoter and I am the star—the star who doesn't twinkle very bright financially…Summing it up, the relationship is comparable to a marriage of convenience with mutual admiration entirely lacking."[3]

Gonzalez and Kramer ended up in court over the issue. The judge sided with Kramer, and Gonzalez headed out on the 1960 tour. This time he beat Alex Olmedo, who had won Wimbledon in 1959, Segura, and Rosewall.

The past decade had placed Gonzalez in an exclusive club. He was the only man to ever become the star on the professional tour after being beaten on his first tour. In every other case, an amateur who turned professional and lost his first tour was never able to rise to star status. Yet Gonzalez did more than achieve top billing. He reached the point at which there could be no tour without him. Without Gonzalez playing, many owners did not want the tour to play in their arena. They did not believe they would make money on ticket sales without him. Pancho Gonzalez had become tennis's greatest attraction.

Gonzalez, who became tennis's greatest attraction, signs autographs for fans.

For the first time in years, Gonzalez did not play in the World Professional Tennis Championships. That year's final round was played by two men Gonzalez had formerly beaten quite soundly—Trabert and Olmedo. Olmedo took home the trophy.

By now Gonzalez had remarried. His new wife's name was Madelyn Darrow. Together they would have three daughters—Christina, Mariessa, and Andrea.

Gonzalez won his final professional tour in 1961, a round robin tour consisting of six players. Spaniard Andres Gimeno, a new touring pro, finished second. Gonzalez was back at the World Professional Tennis Championships that year. He won, making it a record eighth title. This meant that between Segura, Gonzalez, and Olmedo, three Latinos had won the most important professional tennis title for the last twelve years. Gonzalez alone had eight of these.

One expert explained that much of Gonzalez's success stemmed from his attitude. "'Pancho' seldom lets anything bother him for long," he said. "He'll go into the arena before a match and look at the lights—they're bad—and he'll look at the ceiling—there's smoke—and he'll test the court—it's slippery. So he'll shrug his shoulders, figure it's the same for everybody and then go out there and give it a battle."[4]

But now that Gonzalez's contract with Kramer had finally expired he was ready for a break. So he retired from professional competition and moved to Paradise Island in the Bahamas. The island was being developed into a resort. It had tennis courts, a marina, a golf course, and an elegant hotel. Gonzalez was hired to be the resort's head tennis professional. As such, Gonzalez gave lessons to resort visitors. Many of the people who came to his lessons

Gonzalez and his second wife, Madelyn.

were nervous because of his large size and larger reputation. But Gonzalez was a patient teacher. Most people left having been charmed by his gentleness and sense of humor. As for the women, some were overwhelmed by his handsomeness. One even called him "a bronze Greek god."[5]

It was not long before Gonzalez was one of the most popular personalities at the resort. Guests liked talking with him whenever he appeared on the hotel's porch. Gonzalez was usually happy to talk. But he could be temperamental, too. Occasionally he would cancel a lesson with little reason or apology.

One island visitor claimed to notice a pattern in his behavior. According to this visitor, Gonzalez was kindest to the ordinary people who visited the resort. On the other hand, the more well known or pompous a person, the more likely Gonzalez would cancel that individual's lesson.[6]

Gonzalez himself was something of a celebrity. On a tour of the White House in 1962, he was introduced to President John F. Kennedy. The President was an avid sports fan. He asked Gonzalez why Australians dominated recent Davis Cup competitions. The President worried that U.S. talent was weakening. Gonzalez assured President Kennedy that the only problem with the nation's tennis talent was that it was young. Indeed, Australia won the competition in 1962. However, the next year, Gonzalez coached the team and the U.S. captured the Cup.

One member of that team had been Arthur Ashe. Ashe was the first African-American ever named to a U.S. Davis Cup team. He had fought to gain acceptance in the whites-only world of tennis while growing up in Richmond, Virginia. He would soon begin school at the University of California at Los Angeles (UCLA) on a tennis scholarship. At the time, UCLA had one of the most integrated sports programs in the country.

Even so, Ashe still faced discrimination. For example, once he was the only member of UCLA's tennis squad not invited to a tournament at a private California club.[7] This snub left Ashe particularly angry. Fortunately, he had a friend in Los Angeles who understood what he was going through—Richard Gonzalez.

Arthur Ashe, the first African-American man to win the U.S. National Championship, was grateful for the guidance and inspiration he received from his friend Gonzalez.

Ashe had seen Gonzalez play tennis many years earlier in Richmond. He had been impressed with Gonzalez's powerful game and even more impressed by the color of Gonzalez's skin. Seeing someone who had broken through tennis's color barrier inspired Ashe. So when he moved to Los Angeles to attend college, Ashe visited the Los Angeles Tennis Club often to watch Gonzalez practice.

In time the two became friends, and they worked out together. Ashe's game improved under Gonzalez's guidance, and he was grateful for Gonzalez's friendship. He later wrote, "[T]hree stars shone brighter than all the others in my sky. One of them was Pancho Gonzalez, who was not only the best player in the world but also an outsider, like me, because he was Mexican American."[8]

Gonzalez was clearly proud of this heritage. It was around this time that he began using the traditional spelling of his name.

When not coaching Davis Cup teams, Gonzalez often worked on Paradise Island. One pastime there was a game called "Paradise tennis" which the resort's owners had invented. It was a mixture of tennis and ping-pong played on a huge table with a rubber ball and short tennis rackets. It was intended to be played for fun. But as usual, Gonzalez took the competition seriously.

In one tournament, he and Jack Kramer were doubles partners. When their opponents placed a shot close to the net, Gonzalez leaped for it. He landed on the table on his back. His weight bent a table leg, and the table sagged. Somehow, though, Kramer kept the ball in play long enough for Gonzalez to slide off the table and hold it up for Kramer. The two went on to win the match.[9]

While Gonzalez worked on Paradise Island, his wife Madelyn and their daughters stayed at the couple's home in California. Sometimes they flew to the island to visit him. When the resort's tourist season ended, Gonzalez moved back to California.

Gonzalez kept as busy during these vacations from Paradise Island as he did when he was working there. He often held tennis clinics at his California home. He dreamed of finding a youngster to develop into a future champion. Right now he pinned his hopes on his own fourteen-year-old son, Richard Jr. Richard was talented and could even ace his father on occasion, something Gonzalez was proud to note.[10]

In the meantime, the professional tennis tour faltered. There had been no tour in 1962. Kramer's 1963 tour barely survived financially because so few people came to watch the matches. Some felt this was because Gonzalez, whose immense drawing power had kept the tour alive for years, was no longer part of it.

So when the promoters of the 1963 U.S. Professional Grass Court Championships began planning for the tournament at Forest Hills, they believed they needed Gonzalez to attract paying spectators. To get him to enter, they offered him $5,000 in advance. The tournament's first prize was only $1,400. Gonzalez accepted the offer and was the only player to receive any money before the tournament began.[11]

When the other players learned of Gonzalez's unique deal, they were furious. Most refused to talk to him. "They won't even practice with me," Gonzalez reported, "but I'm going to win this tournament."[12]

But while Gonzalez's heart was in the game, his body was not. The out-of-shape champ was matched in the first round against Alex Olmedo. Olmedo was in top condition. Gonzalez lost the first set, then somehow managed to win the second. By the third set, though, Gonzalez was so exhausted he could barely play.

He later remembered how he felt near the end of the match. "My knees were so weak I couldn't stand up and my confidence and swing were also missing. If I hit an approach shot from the service

Gonzalez returns to professional tennis competition briefly in 1963, but is too out of shape to compete at its highest levels.

line, I didn't know if it would hit the bottom of the net or the fence."[13] Gonzalez lost and the tournament went on without him.

In the final round of play, Ken Rosewall beat an up-and-coming Australian, Rod Laver. But by then, the tournament had gone bankrupt and there was no money to pay Rosewall his first-place prize. The champion left with nothing more than a handshake. However, Gonzalez, the first-round loser, walked off with $5,000!

Yet even though he had lost, Gonzalez had enjoyed competing again. So much so, in fact, that he feared he might never win at tennis again. He began training once more. By the time the 1964 U.S. Professional Championships rolled around, the thirty-six-year-old Gonzalez was well conditioned. This time he made it to the final to face Rod Laver.

It had been raining all week, and it was still raining on the morning of their match. But Gonzalez and Laver were required to play. The two slipped and slid across the grass, neither one willing to give up. It took Laver four challenging sets to conquer Gonzalez. Yet Gonzalez left the tournament feeling satisfied that he could still be a top competitor.

Gonzalez also known as the "Big Cat" moved well throughout his career.

And he was. Gonzalez won several other tournaments that year including the U.S. Professional Indoor Championship. At this tournament he defeated Laver, Hoad, and Rosewall on consecutive days. Gonzalez continued to win tournaments, and although he was no longer the best, he was still ranked as one of the top three players in the world.

1 Cy Rice, *Man With a Racket: The Autobiography of Pancho Gonzales* (New York: A. S. Barnes and Company, 1959), p.213.
2 Ibid., p.14.
3 "Pancho on Pancho," *World Tennis*, July 1981, p.46.
4 Walter Bingham, "Champions in Trouble," *Sports Illustrated*, February 6, 1961, p.8.
5 William Brinkley, "The Antic Arts-Pancho Gonzales," *Holiday*, July 1963, p.86.
6 Ibid., p.88.
7 Arthur Ashe, *A Hard Road to Glory* (New York: Amistad Press, Inc., 1993), p.170.
8 Arthur Ashe and Arnold Rampersad, *Days of Grace* (New York: Alfred A. Knopf, 1993), p.61.
9 Rex Lardner, "What's So Funny With Pancho?" *Sports Illustrated*, July 31, 1961, p.27.
10 Brinkley, p.93.
11 Walter Bingham, "A Legend Dies on the Court," *Sports Illustrated*, July 8, 1963, p.19.
12 Ibid.
13 Pancho Gonzalez, "That Period of Adjustment," *World Tennis*, August 1987, p.80.

The Name of the Game Is Strategy

In 1968, Gonzalez's twenty years in tennis were honored when he was inducted into the International Tennis Hall of Fame at the Newport Casino in Newport, Rhode Island. This placed him in impressive company. Fifty-two other players had already been inducted, including Bill Tilden, Ellsworth Vines, Fred Perry, Don Budge, and Jack Kramer.

Gonzalez was the first person of color to make it to the Hall of Fame.[1] In addition, he was the first player ever inducted while still a top competitor. The others had not been honored until many years after they had retired.

The honor seemed appropriate. People who had never played tennis before tried the sport after reading about Gonzalez's matches or seeing him compete. During the 1950s, there was a massive increase in tennis participation on public courts. By the end of the sixties, huge numbers of tennis enthusiasts came in all colors and from all economic backgrounds.

In 1968, Gonzalez was inducted into the International Tennis Hall of Fame. Today, he is honored along with other champions in the Grand Slam Gallery.

In 1968, tennis officials added more excitement to the sport's increasing popularity. They opened major tennis tournaments like Wimbledon to both amateur and professional players. For the first time ever all players could compete against each other. This is known as open tennis.

Gonzalez had supported open tennis since the late 1950s. But when he spoke of open tennis, Gonzalez always added one exception. He hoped that the Davis Cup competition would remain an amateur event. Gonzalez felt that this particular competition should be played for national honor rather than for money.

As for tournament tennis, Gonzalez believed that opening up the sport would be healthy. It would allow more players to earn money. In addition, it would bring more competition to the sport, improving everyone's play. Gonzalez had waited a long time for open tennis, and he was anxious to be a part of it.

Others were not as eager. With more players competing against each other, some professionals feared that their own earnings would decrease. Many also suspected that open tennis would be bad for their win-loss records. Their worries seemed logical.

During the previous decade, a small number of professionals had competed against each other often. They knew each other's playing styles well. This meant they could develop a game strategy based on their own strengths and their particular opponent's weaknesses.

But open tennis would increase the number of players competing, and most amateurs were unknown to the current professionals. This would make it difficult for them to develop pre-game strategies and could mean losses for the professionals. Gonzalez understood this danger, but he still looked forward to open play.

The first open tournament was held in Bournemouth, England, in April 1968. In the second round Gonzalez faced amateur Mark Cox, an Englishman who was considered the underdog. Hundreds of English spectators had come to cheer for Cox. But as the match progressed, many people discovered the irresistible lure of Richard Gonzalez.

The admiring crowd could not help the thirty-nine-year-old Gonzalez win, though. Although he took all six games of the first set, he lost the second set. He won the third set by two games but lost the fourth. During a short break, Gonzalez changed shoes that were waterlogged with sweat. It did not help. As the two began the fifth and deciding set, Cox was strong and confident, but Gonzalez was tired. This was the first five-set match he had played in several years.

Cox won the fifth set, making Richard Gonzalez the first professional player ever to be beaten by an amateur. After the historic event, reporters followed Gonzalez into the locker room for an interview. Most expected one of his trademark temper tantrums and waited guardedly for him to erupt. But Gonzalez was tired, not angry. "Somebody had to be the first to lose to an amateur. It might as well be me," he told them. "I was glad to be a part of this. Didn't think I'd ever see it happen. Now let me take a shower. I've been working pretty hard."[2]

Next came the French Open. This time Gonzalez made it to the semi-finals before being eliminated. This was a tremendous feat considering that the French tournament is played on clay, a surface that requires great stamina. The ball bounces slower and stays in play longer on clay.

Then came Wimbledon. Ironically, in twenty years of tennis, this was only the second time Gonzalez had played there. The first time had been in 1949 and it had ended in an earlier-than-expected loss. On this second trip, Gonzalez, now forty, lost again. He felt he played poorly because he was nervous.

After Wimbledon, Gonzalez began training seriously for September's U.S. Open. There he played with such determination that he beat the number two seed, Tony Roche, to advance to the quarterfinals. One observer noted that only someone who wanted very badly to win could work so hard for so long. Gonzalez lost in the next round. Even so, *Newsweek* magazine reported that his performance had been the highlight of the tournament.[3]

In 1969, Gonzalez traveled back to Wimbledon for a third time. On this visit he won one of the most dramatic matches in tennis history. In the first round, forty-one-year-old Gonzalez faced twenty-five-year-old Puerto Rican Charlie Pasarell. Pasarell had won the U.S. National Indoor title earlier in the year by beating Arthur Ashe.

The first set began late in the afternoon and ended with Gonzalez losing 24–22. After more than two hours of play, daylight was beginning to fade. Because of his age Gonzalez was having trouble seeing the ball. He asked the umpire several times to postpone the match

**Gonzalez plays Charlie Pasarell on Wimbledon's Centre Court
in one of the greatest tennis matches of all time.**

until the next day. His request was denied each time. This infuriated Gonzalez. He cursed the darkness and ranted at the umpire.

He was so angry that he barely tried during the second set and lost 6–1. At that point the officials finally stopped play until the following day. Gonzalez walked off the court and threw his racket at the umpire's chair. Fans booed his angry behavior, making Gonzalez one of the few players ever to be booed off a Wimbledon court.

Back in his hotel room, Gonzalez was too angry to sleep. He and Madelyn played backgammon until two in the morning. Even so, the next day Gonzalez walked onto the court ready to play. Unfortunately, he had already lost the first two sets of the match.

Yet Gonzalez was not ready to concede defeat. During the next two hours, the lead went back and forth as an astonished crowd watched Gonzalez fight back. A few people even began encouraging him. The number grew with each point he won. Gonzalez took the third set 16–14. Then he tied the match by winning the fourth set.

Now anticipation swept through the Centre Court and all thirteen thousand fans seemed to be rooting for Gonzalez. They cheered each time he won a point. They groaned whenever he lost one. Echoing the sounds of the spectators on the inside, several thousand people tracked his progress on a scoreboard outside the stadium.

Finally it seemed that the great match was coming to an end. Pasarell was ahead in the fifth set, 5–4. Gonzalez was down love–40 on his serve. If Pasarell won any of the next three points, he would win the match. Gonzalez won the next point. Then another and another. Time after time, just when Gonzalez seemed doomed, he managed to stay alive. When the set finally ended in an amaz-

Gonzalez and Pasarell leave the Centre Court after their epic encounter.

ing 11–9 victory for Gonzalez, the crowd exploded in cheers and applause.

As for Gonzalez, he was too tired to show much emotion. He and Pasarell walked to the net and embraced as spectators gave the men a reverberating ovation. They both had played magnificently in a record-setting five-hour, twelve-minute, 112-game match.

In the locker room Pasarell found a corner where he sat down and cried. Gonzalez sat next to him and put his arm around him. He told Pasarell that he was sorry.[4] But Pasarell was not mad at Gonzalez. Pasarell had idolized Gonzalez for many years. His remarkable play had simply raised Pasarell's esteem for him another notch.

Pasarell called Gonzalez's serve the best he had ever seen. He went on to say that Gonzalez "was a guy who would never give up. Somehow he would figure out how to win a match."[5]

Gonzalez advanced in the tournament until he lost to Ashe in the fourth round of action. Rod Laver won the tournament. Laver's win was as remarkable as Gonzalez's victory over Pasarell. It was Laver's second win in a row at Wimbledon, and Laver was on his way to becoming the first player ever to win the Grand Slam twice. His first Grand Slam had been in 1962. By winning Wimbledon in 1969, he had three of the four victories necessary to do it again.

But Laver's amazing accomplishment at Wimbledon in 1969 was overshadowed in many news reports by Gonzalez's victory over Pasarell there. Laver was not surprised. He commented, "That's Pancho for you, always stealing the show."[6] Even today when play at Wimbledon is stopped due to rain, audiences are often entertained by a broadcast of the Gonzalez-Pasarell match.

Laver completed his second Grand Slam by beating Tony Roche in the 1969 U.S. final at Forest Hills. No other player has ever won two Grand Slams. As a result, many consider Laver to be the greatest player that ever lived.

Yet many experts believe it was the rules rather than skill that kept Gonzalez from accomplishing Laver's feat. As a professional, he could not compete in Grand Slam tournaments for almost twenty years. Many people feel that if open tennis had come earlier, Gonzalez would certainly hold the record for the most Grand Slam titles won. As proof of their claim, they note that when he did face Laver in competition, Gonzalez was well past his prime. Nonetheless, he often beat Laver, even in his forties.

Next Gonzalez went into training for the 1969 U.S. Open. He smoked less, watched his weight, and played tennis all day long. He also rested. This was a much more conscientious approach to conditioning than Gonzalez had practiced in his younger years. But Gonzalez knew that his age demanded better physical preparation.

One writer wrote that the most important part of Gonzalez's training program was getting himself in the mood to fight. Gonzalez retreated, the writer said, "to dwell on his resentments... and work himself into a mean, sullen mood, because that's the way he plays best."[7] Gonzalez responded by saying, "I've always fought, because I've always been pushed around."[8]

Although age was affecting Gonzalez's physical prowess, it was not dulling his determination. In fact, it seemed that Gonzalez fought harder now than ever before and that winning had become an obsession. Gonzalez explained his attitude differently. He said that open tennis had brought new competition to tennis, and he wanted to be a part of it.

Age had not detracted from Gonzalez's charisma either. His jet-black hair was graying, but he was still slim and fit. His court presence remained overpowering. As one writer observed, "Women find him fascinating when he steps on the court, gaunt and sinister, and begins stalking his prey. Men are intrigued by his hoodlum appeal, his angry and sullen manner."[9]

The organizers of the 1969 U.S. Open were fully aware of Gonzalez's crowd appeal. They expected Gonzalez to draw large numbers of spectators, so they scheduled his matches in the stadium where there was the most seating. In the meantime, higher-ranked players competed on the outside courts.

Gonzalez easily beat his opponents during the first two rounds of play. In the third round he was trailing Torben Ulrich two sets to one, when the players took a break. Gonzalez's feet hurt and his legs ached. For a few moments, he thought about retiring, saying he felt a hundred years old. Then he walked back on the court and won the match.

Part of Gonzalez's secret to success in his later years was game strategy. He was able to analyze opponents' games and was known as a master tactician. Here he is shown with Clark Graebner, who achieved a No. 2 U.S. and No. 7 world ranking in 1968.

Gonzalez lost in the next round. He was forty-one years old, and his age could not be denied in the physically grueling world of championship tennis. His back became stiff and his nervous energy gave him stomach aches. In addition, his eyes seemed to be getting worse. Gonzalez wore glasses for reading and watching television, but he would not wear them for tennis. When he did, he had difficulty telling exactly where the ball was. Instead he took mineral tablets that he felt helped his vision. When a reporter asked him why he kept playing, Gonzalez replied, "Because I'm not smart, that is why. I like to punish myself."[10]

But Gonzalez was not about to quit playing because of aches and pains. Instead he found ways to overcome them. He practiced daily to keep his body in condition. He used an aluminum racket because it was lighter than wood. This enabled him to gain fractions of a second in speed. He cut the pockets out of his tennis shorts to get rid of the extra weight they created when they were wet with sweat. Gonzalez also stayed calmer on the court, knowing that anger burns up energy.

Gonzalez's most powerful weapon, though, was his mind. Hoping to wear down an opponent, he looked for each one's weakness and played to it. He had always outsmarted opponents before. Now he honed strategy to an art form. Many players described Gonzalez as having the best tactical expertise of anyone in the game. As for Gonzalez, he said he would rather have the energy of a youngster than all the knowledge in the world.

Yet he won the 1969 Pacific Southwest Tournament. Next came the Howard Hughes Open in Las Vegas, where Gonzalez conquered the world's sixth-ranked John Newcombe and third-ranked Rosewall to work his way to the final.

Opposite Gonzalez was the second-ranked Arthur Ashe. Gonzalez seemed to be on fire during this match. He made one perfectly placed shot after another. Ashe even applauded Gonzalez after one outstanding stroke.[11] Gonzalez defeated Ashe 6–0, 6–2, 6–4 to win the tournament.

Gonzalez had begun that year ranked tenth in the world tennis standings. He finished it ranked number six.

Then Gonzalez announced another retirement. During the past decade he and Madelyn had been divorced. Now the two were remarried. Gonzalez wanted to spend more time with her and their children. He also wanted to devote his energy to developing a tennis camp at his home in Malibu.

Even so, Gonzalez entered a series of "winner-take-all" matches in 1970. In the first contest he faced the now two-time Grand Slam winner Rod Laver. More than 15,000 fans came to Madison Square Garden in New York City to watch.

In 1970, forty-two-year-old Gonzalez defeats 1969 Grand Slam champion Rod Laver in front of 15,000 fans at Madison Square Garden in New York.

Gonzalez knew strategy would play a major role in this match. Laver was only five feet seven inches—not very tall as tennis players went. Gonzalez decided to use this to his advantage. As often as he could, when Laver advanced to the net, Gonzalez lobbed the ball over Laver's head and out of his reach. During the final two sets, his game plan began to pay off. After hitting Laver lob after lob that dropped just inches beyond his reach, Gonzalez surprised him with powerful low drives across the net. Using this strategy, the old warrior was able to beat Laver in five hard-fought sets and earn the $10,000 winner's purse. A week later Gonzalez won another $10,000 by beating John Newcombe, who would win Wimbledon later that year.

In 1971, Gonzalez entered the Pacific Southwest Tournament where he worked his way to the final. There he met up-and-coming young Jimmy Connors. But youth held no advantage, and Gonzalez beat the seventeen-year-old to win the tournament.

Although Gonzalez was forty-three years old and supposedly in the twilight of his career, one writer observed of him, "somehow the sun never quite sets."[12] But not even Richard Gonzalez could keep the sun from setting.

1 Bud Collins and Zander Hollander, *Bud Collins' Modern Encyclopedia of Tennis* (New York: Doubleday and Company, 1980), pp.240–251.
2 Bud Collins, *My Life With the Pros* (New York: E.P. Dutton, 1989), p.195.
3 "Pancho Turns Them On," *Newsweek*, September 16, 1968, p.62.
4 Thomas Bonk, "Pancho Gonzalez, One of Tennis' Greatest Stars, Dies," *Los Angeles Times*, July 5, 1995, p.A12.
5 Paul Bauman, "Gonzalez's Talent Matched By Tenacity," *Las Vegas Review-Journal*, July 5, 1995, p.3E.
6 Collins, p.126.
7 Marshall Smith, "This Old Pro Is Just Too Mean to Quit," *Life*, September 12, 1969, p.77.
8 Ibid., p.79.
9 Ibid., p.78.
10 Ibid., p.79.
11 "Adios, Pancho," *Newsweek*, October 20, 1969, p.105.
12 Kim Chapin, "El Pancho Grande," *Sports Illustrated*, July 7, 1969, p.57.

The Old Wolf

Richard Gonzalez's name dropped permanently from World Top Ten tennis rankings in 1970. He had been a tough competitor for over twenty years, but now younger men would take his place. As they did, tennis experienced an unprecedented growth in popularity.

One cause of this great boom was open tennis. With more money-making possibilities, more players than ever before were entering tournaments. This meant more tournaments were held. More tournaments brought increased exposure of the sport, which in turn brought in more recreational players.

New tennis players needed to buy equipment and clothing for their latest hobby. This made the advertising of tennis products profitable. Advertisements increased people's exposure to the sport and produced more tennis fans. Thus, open tennis created an ever-increasing number of tennis enthusiasts.

All these new tennis players needed places to play. So during the 1970s city parks everywhere seemed to overflow with people wanting to use a tennis court. New courts were built, and public recreation programs now included tennis lessons and tournaments.

In addition, television began broadcasting a lot more tournaments. These broadcasts brought large audiences, making advertising during the telecasts profitable. Sponsoring a tournament brought even greater advertising opportunities—the bigger the tournament, the bigger the benefit. Consequently, a few corporations began organizing tournaments with huge cash prizes.

Of course, only the very best players made it to the final rounds of these tournaments. But those who did earned the largest prizes ever. Between 1950 and 1970, Richard Gonzalez had won close to one million dollars playing tennis. However, in 1974 alone, four different players earned $200,000 each in winnings. By the end of the decade, the best players were earning close to one million dollars a year. This was in prize money alone. In addition, many earned even more money by endorsing products.

Although Gonzalez did not share in the wealth open tennis brought, he was happy to have played a part in bringing about the explosion in tennis's popularity. He once reported, "I'm satisfied to know I was one of the pioneers, one of the guys who made the tennis boom possible."[1]

Undoubtedly, Gonzalez had been a crucial part of tennis's increase in popularity. He had brought raw power, emotion, and excitement to a game often thought to be a refined pastime rather than a demanding sport. Anyone who watched Gonzalez play a set or two saw the tremendous athleticism and stamina needed to perform at tennis's top level.

Furthermore, Gonzalez represented the underdog in American society. He had risen to the top of the sport without ever having had a formal lesson from a professional. Gonzalez was an outsider who

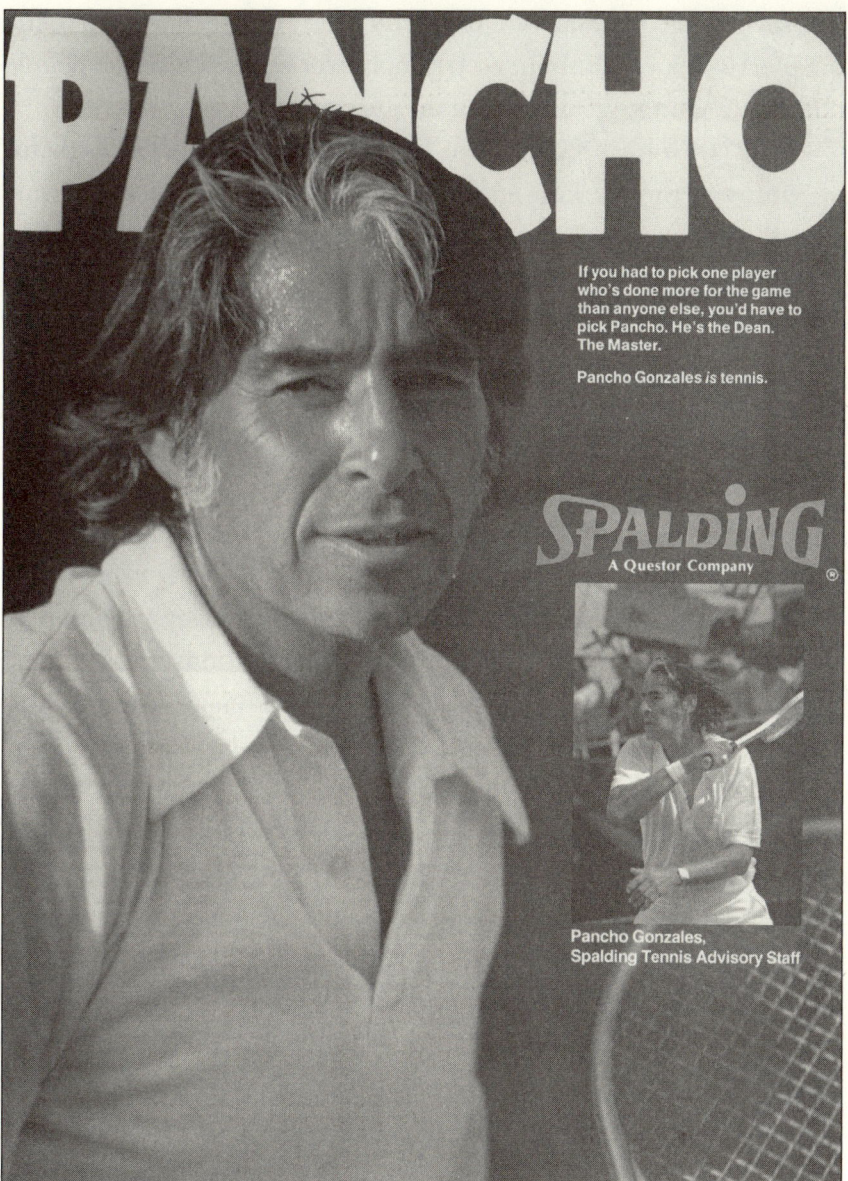

Pancho was a great contributor to the sport of tennis.

had succeeded through hard work and a fiery desire to win. To many people, Gonzalez symbolized triumph over adversity. Some people credit him with revolutionizing the sport.

In 1971, Gonzalez moved to Las Vegas to work as the Director of Tennis at the world-famous hotel Caesars Palace. By 1972, his second marriage to Madelyn Darrow had ended in divorce. In December, Gonzalez married Betty Steward. They would have a daughter named Jeanna.

During 1973, Gonzalez played in a series of tennis tournaments called the Grand Masters. The Grand Masters Tour was designed for men over the age of forty-five who had once been the best tennis players in the world. Gonzalez had already competed against most of them—players such as Pancho Segura, Frank Sedgman, Alex Olmedo, and Mal Anderson.

This tour gave the old professionals a chance to stay fit and play tennis against opponents of equal skill. The atmosphere among the players was friendly and nostalgic. They often gathered to play poker, socialize, and reminisce.

Unlike in the old days when Gonzalez had stayed to himself, he now attended the parties they held. In fact, he was often the first one there and treated his old comrades to drinks. Many of these men noticed a marked change in Gonzalez since his days on the professional circuit. Now, they said, he was much more easygoing and social. According to Laver, Gonzalez was mellowing.[2]

But the athletic Gonzalez remained alive and well. On the court, Gonzalez was a tough opponent and frequent winner. His serves were still amazingly fast, and he played in his characteristic cat-like crouch. In addition, he demonstrated the same passion for winning he had shown in his younger days. Amid the genteel atmosphere of the Grand Masters Tour, Gonzalez sometimes lost his temper and shouted at an official or opponent.

Gonzalez continued to complete on the Grand Masters tour. Tennis became a lifelong sport he played until the final months of his life.

Even non-tournament matches could be fierce competitions to Gonzalez. Once a bystander heard him challenge a friend to "suicide singles." When he asked Gonzalez what this meant, Gonzalez replied, "If he beats me, I'll cut my throat."[3]

Now Gonzalez had assumed a new role, the role of the aging expert. People called him the "Old Wolf" and looked to him for advice about their own tennis games.

In 1978, Gonzalez published another book. This one was called *Tennis Begins At Forty.* In this book, Gonzalez gave tips for a different kind of tennis from what he had played most of his life. He described how adults new to the game or adults over the age of forty could play good tennis and have fun. Gonzalez himself claimed to enjoy the sport more now than in the days when he was constantly competing.

He also wrote articles for tennis magazines. Some gave advice. Others expressed his views on the sport. In one he gave tips for longevity in tennis. "An athlete should learn how to rest more while he's competing," Gonzalez advised. "Players don't realize that the body needs rest...Invariably, they'll lie down after practice for 10 or 15 minutes and then wake up and find a couple of hours have gone by. Your body is talking to you. The same thing is true before and after a match. Proper rest is crucial to good preparation."[4]

Gonzalez had become more health-conscious in other ways, too. In the early 1980s he quit smoking. He also developed a taste for the sport he had once described as dull—golf. He believed tennis and golf were a good combination for keeping his body in top shape.

Gonzalez also believed in keeping his mind sharp. He still loved racing and working on his cars. Solving their mechanical problems

Racing became a lifelong activity. Here Gonzalez's beautiful 1956 Thunderbird leaves the starting line at the Las Vegas Drag Strip.

and making them faster was a mental challenge he enjoyed. In addition, he read every day.

Over the years, Gonzalez had come to understand why Perry Jones had been so adamant about his staying in school. He wished he had listened to Jones and all the others who had urged him to complete his education. Gonzalez encouraged the youth he worked with to complete theirs. He also encouraged them to read daily, just as he did. He believed that keeping the mind in shape was just as important as keeping the body in shape.

Keeping his personal life in top shape was more difficult. Gonzalez was now divorced from Betty Steward and married to a woman named Cheryl Duff.

At about this time, another change was taking place in tennis. It was led by men such as John McEnroe, Jimmy Connors, and Ilie Nastase. These new champions displayed court manners worse than anyone had ever seen before. McEnroe was dubbed "Superbrat," Connors was called vulgar, and Nastase racked up fine after fine for unsportsmanlike behavior.

Gonzalez, who was once famous for his rants at officials, was asked about the behavior of tennis's newest stars. "I think it's terrible," he said, "but I'm the wrong one to say so."[5] Yet Gonzalez felt there was a difference between his own court antics and the latest lapses in etiquette. He explained, "I got angry myself, but it was to make me play better. If I cursed a line call, I did it quietly, for no one else to hear. This other stuff—the gestures, the four-letter words—it shows a lack of maturity. It reflects on the stupidity of the individual who, I guess, has no respect for his fellow man."[6]

Sometimes Gonzalez played tennis with his oldest son Richard Jr. They entered father-and-son doubles tournaments and won a few national titles.

Gonzalez also kept active in Davis Cup happenings. This competition continued to be special to him since it was played for the country's honor, not just the honor of the individuals involved. As Gonzalez pointed out, at the end of a winning match the umpire does not say, "Game, Gonzalez." He says, "Game, United States."[7]

Gonzalez attended Davis Cup competitions when he could. In 1981, he watched his old friend Arthur Ashe captain a U.S. team. During a break, Gonzalez advised Ashe to be more involved in what was happening on the court.

Ashe protested to his former mentor, saying that he was involved. Sometimes, he told Gonzalez, he was so worried about the play that his heart was pounding. Gonzalez replied, "Well, we don't want your heart to thump too much, Arthur. But you have to look more involved, I guess."[8]

Being involved was something Gonzalez had done all of his life. Now he expressed unhappiness with the way Davis Cup play had become a moneymaking event. Gonzalez felt this was ruining its value.[9]

Another aspect of Davis Cup play bothered Gonzalez. Because of the recent poor behavior of tennis players, the United States Tennis Association (the former USLTA) had written a code of conduct for Davis Cup team members. Any person who wanted to play on the team had to agree to follow its guidelines.

Some of the U.S.'s best players did not like this new requirement. John McEnroe refused to sign the statement although he said he would abide by the code. And even thought Gonzalez did not like McEnroe's behavior on the court, he supported his decision. He said, "I wouldn't even give it a second thought. Under those terms, I would not play Davis Cup. I don't think anyone should dictate conditions on what I'm doing as a player."[10] Gonzalez saw the USTA requirement of signing an oath as hypocritical and unrealistic. To him, the members were setting standards that they themselves could not live by.

By 1984, Gonzalez had divorced Cheryl Duff and married Rita Agassi, sister of tennis star Andre Agassi. Rita was his fifth wife and a talented player herself. They often played tennis together. In 1985, Rita and Gonzalez became the parents of Gonzalez's eighth child, his son Skylar.

When Gonzalez's contract with Caesars Palace expired in 1986, he began holding tennis clinics in the Bahamas, Hawaii, Palm Springs, and other resort locations.

Rita and Skylar often traveled with him. For the first time in his life, Gonzalez was able to spend long periods of time with one of his children. He liked this new role and was more patient with Skylar than he had been with his other children. Consequently, he and Skylar became very close. Gonzalez's marital relationship was more difficult. In 1989, he and Rita were divorced.

Gonzalez continued to play tennis. Occasionally he appeared in a senior tournament, and as before, he drew a large crowd. But now people did not come to see Gonzalez's brilliant shots or his relentless grit. They came to see the legendary player who had defeated so many tennis greats.

---

1 "Pancho on Pancho," *World Tennis*, July 1981, p.46.
2 Paul Bauman, "Gonzalez Mourned At Service," *Las Vegas Review-Journal*, July 9, 1995, p.5A.
3 John Sharnik, *Remembrance of Games Past* (New York: MacMillan Publishing Company, 1986), pp.259–260.
4 Pancho Gonzalez, "That Period of Adjustment," *World Tennis*, August 1987, p.80.
5 Sharnik, p.259.
6 "Pancho on Pancho," p.46.
7 Alan Trengove, *The Story of the Davis Cup* (London: Stanley Paul, 1985), p.5.
8 Arthur Ashe and Arnold Rampersad, *Days of Grace* (New York: Alfred A. Knopf, 1993), p.70.
9 Richard "Pancho" Gonzalez, "Freedom of Choice and the Davis Cup," *World Tennis*, August 1985, p.80.
10 Ibid.

Tennis's Best

In the fall of 1994, Gonzalez learned that he had cancer of the esophagus. The cancer began spreading in the spring of 1995. By summer it was out of control and Gonzalez was in terrible pain. He was hospitalized just as Wimbledon began.

Yet Gonzalez was not about to miss the world's most important tennis tournament. He watched the matches on television, playing each game in his mind as if he were there.

Gonzalez paid particular attention to Andre Agassi's matches. Gonzalez had once said that Agassi was a better player than he had ever been. But now as he watched Agassi, he was not so sure. In addition to his powerhouse serve, Gonzalez knew that he had once had remarkable speed and an outstanding variety of shots.

Gonzalez began thinking that he may have beaten Agassi had they met when he was in top condition. In fact, Gonzalez said, "The more I watch [today's players], the more I think they're not that great. They're good, but not as good as I was."[1]

In 2005, *Tennis* magazine chose Gonzalez as the greatest server of all time.

Richard Gonzalez died at the age of sixty-seven on Monday, July 3, 1995. Two hundred people attended his funeral. Many came to say good-bye to the man who had been their brother, father, or grandfather. Others came to honor a colleague and friend. Among these were Charlie Pasarell, Dennis Ralston, and Rod Laver. "You knew you were in for a battle every time you played him," Laver recalled. "He never let you off with any cheap points."[2]

Laver was not the only one who would remember Gonzalez's superb tennis skills. In 1999, *Sports Illustrated* magazine selected Gonzalez as one of the top twenty favorite athletes of the 20th century. In 2005, *Tennis* magazine chose him as the greatest server of all time.

Many fans and experts believe that Gonzalez would have won Wimbledon eight or nine times if it had been open to professionals before 1968. In fact, Gonzalez is often referred to as the greatest tennis player never to have won Wimbledon.

Like the fans of other sports, tennis lovers enjoy comparing great players from various eras. For example, they might wonder who was a better player at his peak—Jack Kramer or John McEnroe. Two years before Gonzalez's death, *Tennis Week* magazine had published an article about this kind of a contest. In the magazine's fantasy tournament among the thirty-two greatest male players in history, Gonzalez beat Don Budge for the title.

When the experts compile their lists of the best players from history, many place Richard Gonzalez at the top. Jimmy Connors once said that if he had to choose someone to play for his life, he would choose Gonzalez.[3]

Gonzalez's athletic skills were awesome and his knowledge of the game precise. But these attributes were only a part of his winning formula. Bobby Riggs believed Gonzalez's greatness was due to something more than magnificent skills. He once said, "I think of [Gonzalez] as the prime example of a man with the burning desire that produces victories. [Gonzalez] at his best had a tremendous serve, true, but he never had the best mechanical game. He was not a penetrating volleyer, he didn't punch the ball with power the way Frank Sedgman or Tony Trabert did, or Ken Rosewall does off his backhand. Any number of players hit the ball harder than [Gonzalez] did off the volley...But no one ever burned with a greater desire to win, and that is what has kept [Gonzalez] in the top ranks of players for a quarter century."[4]

Gonzalez's brother Ralph agreed. Ralph knew how much his brother hated to lose, saying, "He wanted to play better than anyone else ever did."[5] Richard Gonzalez may just have succeeded.

---

1 Paul Bauman, "Gonzalez's Talent Matched By Tenacity," *Las Vegas Review-Journal*, July 5, 1995, p.3E.
2 Paul Bauman, "Gonzalez Mourned At Service," *Las Vegas Review-Journal*, July 9, 1995, p.5A.
3 Andrea Leand, "The Lone Wolf," *Tennis Week*, July 20, 1995, p.36.
4 Bobby Riggs, *Court Hustler* (New York: J.B. Lippincott Company, 1973), p.119.
5 Bauman, "Gonzalez's Talent Matched By Tenacity," p.1E.

Afterword

Richard Gonzalez's greatness went beyond the tennis court. He was the son of Mexican immigrants, a child from a working-class home, and the victim of hurtful discrimination. Yet he overcame these obstacles to make a permanent place for himself in tennis history. Gonzalez's success is proof of what someone with determination and talent can do.

After Gonzalez's death, his brother Ralph pursued a goal of his own. Ralph wanted to tell Richard's story to young people. He wanted them to see that they, too, could reach goals through persistence and hard work. Ralph especially wanted to tell youth from poor families or diverse backgrounds that it was possible to achieve their dreams. So he decided to create a documentary movie of his brother's life. Sadly, Ralph died shortly after work on the documentary began. Ralph's son, Greg, and other family members, however, believed in the importance of the project. They helped complete the work Ralph had started. "Pancho Gonzalez: The Latino Legend of Tennis" premiered at the 2005 Wimbledon Championships. It

Ralph and Richard.

was then shown on Spike TV the following September. Today the documentary is shown to young people everywhere, with hopes that the champion tennis player will inspire them to work toward their own goals.

As for Richard Gonzalez, he never saw himself as a role model. He simply became the best tennis player he could be. And in so doing, he became a testimonial to the value of perseverance and hard work, and a symbol of hope to anyone with a dream.

Chronology

1928: Richard Alonzo Gonzales is born in Los Angeles, California, on May 9.

1940: Richard's mother gives him a tennis racket for Christmas. He soon becomes an avid tennis player who learns the sport by watching others play.

1943: Richard plays in various tournaments to become the number one boy's 15 and under in Southern California tennis.

1945: Richard enlists in the United States Navy.

1947: After being discharged from the Navy, Gonzalez places well in the Southern California Men's Tennis Championships. He then plays in a series of tournaments, including the U.S. National Championships.

1948: Gonzalez is suspended from tennis tournaments for the first six months of the year. He marries Henrietta Pedrin, also of Los Angeles. The couple will have three sons. Gonzalez wins the U.S. Clay Court Championship and the U.S. National Championship.

1949: Gonzalez wins the U.S. Indoor Championship on wood, U.S. Clay Court Championship, and U.S. National Championship on grass, becoming the first player in history to hold all three of these titles simultaneously. After winning the U.S. National Championship for the second time he turns professional.

1950: Gonzalez loses his first professional tour against Jack Kramer. As a result, he is not invited on the tour for three years. He wins the Philadelphia Pro Championship and the Wembley Professional Championship.

1951: Gonzalez wins the Wembley Professional Championship.

1952: Gonzalez wins the Wembley Professional Championship and the Philadelphia Pro Round Robin tournament.

1953: Gonzalez wins the World Professional Tennis Championship (a.k.a. the U.S. Professional Championship) and the Wembley Professional Championship.

1954: Gonzalez is invited back on the professional tennis tour. He consistently beats Pancho Segura, Frank Sedgman, and Don Budge to win the tour. Gonzalez also wins the World U.S. Professional Tennis Championship and Wembley Professional Championship.

1955–1956: Gonzalez wins two more World Professional Tennis Championship titles and defeats Tony Trabert 74–27 matches on the world professional tour. He earns a reputation as a ferocious and short-tempered opponent on the court.

1957: Gonzalez wins another World Professional Tennis Championship title. He defeats Ken Rosewall 50–26 matches on the world professional tour.

1958: Gonzalez defeats Lew Hoad 51–36 matches on the world professional tour and in the final of the World Professional Tennis Championship to win his sixth such title. Gonzalez and Henrietta divorce.

1959: Gonzalez wins overall round robin tour, which included Lew Hoad, Mal Anderson and Ashley Cooper. He wins his seventh World Professional Tennis Championship title, beating Hoad in the final.

1960: Gonzalez wins another pro tour defeating Segura, Rosewall and Alex Olmedo and then retires for six months. He does not play in the World Professional Tennis Championships. He marries Madelyn Darrow, with whom he will have three daughters.

1961: Gonzalez wins his final professional tour, a six man round robin tour. He also wins his eighth World Professional Tennis Championship. Gonzalez retires from competitive play to teach tennis at the Paradise Island resort in the Bahamas.

1963: Gonzalez begins coaching the United States Davis Cup team. He attempts a comeback at the U.S. Professional Championships and loses in the first round.

1964–1967: Gonzalez returns to competitive tennis, winning several professional tournaments including the 1964 U.S. Pro Indoor Championship and the 1965 CBS Tennis Championship. In 1966 Gonzalez wins the BBC 2 Trophy tournament at Wembley, England, defeating Ken Rosewall and Rod Laver the same night.

1968: Gonzalez is inducted into the International Tennis Hall of Fame. Now 40 years old, he also becomes the first professional player to lose to an amateur, in tennis's first open tournament.

1969: In a dramatic first round match at Wimbledon, Gonzalez beats Charlie Pasarell in a record-setting five-hour twelve-minute 112-game match. Later in the year Gonzalez wins the Howard Hughes Open in Las Vegas, beating Newcombe, Rosewall and Ashe.

1970: Forty-two-year-old Gonzalez defeats 1969 Grand Slam winner Rod Laver in a $10,000 winner-take-all match at Madison Square Garden in five sets. Later that year he defeats Rod Laver to win the Howard Hughes Open.

1971: Gonzalez retires from tennis competition and moves to Las Vegas to become the teaching pro at Caesars Palace. He wins the Pacific Southwest Tournament in Los Angeles defeating Jimmy Connors in the final.

1972: Gonzalez marries Betty Steward. They will have one daughter. He wins a professional tournament in Des Moines, Iowa, becoming the oldest player ever to win a professional tournament, beating France's Georges Goven at the age of 44 in five sets, having lost the first two.

1973: Gonzalez is invited on the Grand Masters Tour, a new tour for the best professional players from years past. During the next two decades, the aging Gonzalez continues to play in other senior events. In addition, he writes about the sport in tennis magazines.

1983: By now Gonzalez is divorced from Betty Steward and has married and divorced a fourth wife, Cheryl Duff.

1984: Gonzalez marries Andre Agassi's sister, Rita.

1985: Gonzalez's eighth and last child is born.

1986: After leaving his job as Director of Tennis at Caesars Palace, Gonzalez conducts tennis clinics in various resort locations.

1989: Rita Agassi and Gonzalez are divorced. He continues to play tennis regularly and adds golf to his pastimes.

1994: Gonzalez is diagnosed with cancer of the esophagus.

1995: Gonzalez is hospitalized when the cancer spreads. He dies on July 3.

Index